Gender Gaps

◆

Gender Gaps

Where Schools Still Fail Our Children

By the American Association
of University Women

MARLOWE & COMPANY • NEW YORK

Published by
Marlowe & Company
841 Broadway, Fourth Floor
New York, NY 10003

Library of Congress Cataloging-in-Publication Data

Gender gaps : where schools still fail our children / commissioned by
    the American Association of University Women Educational Foundation
    as a follow-up to the book How schools shortchange girls : researched
    by the American Institutes for Research.
        p.   cm.
    Includes bibliographical references (p.) and index.
    ISBN 1-56924-665-3
    1. Women—Education—United States.   2. Educational equaliza-
    tion—United States.   3. Educational change—United States.   4. How
    schools shortchange girls.   I. American Association of University
    Women. Educationl Foundation.   II. American Institutes for Research.
    LC1752.G46   1999
    371.822—dc21   98-43991
                                                                   CIP

Manufactured in the United States of America

TABLE OF CONTENTS

LIST OF TABLES

The American Association of University Women Educational Foundation observed in the early 1990s that girls' needs were not adequately represented or addressed in educational reform. This glaring absence raised several questions: How were girls faring in U.S. public schools? What was girls' experience in the classroom? Was our public education system really equitable?

To answer these questions, the Foundation commissioned the Wellesley College Center for Research on Women to synthesize and analyze more than 1,000 articles and studies on girls and K–12 education. *The AAUW Report: How Schools Shortchange Girls*, first published in 1992, documented disturbing evidence that girls receive an inequitable education, both in quality and quantity, compared to that of boys.

How Schools Shortchange Girls catalyzed local, state, and national action to provide equitable treatment for girls in public schools. Today, few conversations about gender and education in the academic and research communities proceed without mention of the watershed report.

Six years later, research in this area has grown exponentially and occupies a central place in much of the educational reform literature. Even more important, the report prompted numerous efforts to improve educational practices for all students in public schools.

On the eve of the 21st century, what is different today for girls in America's public schools? In 1997 the AAUW Educational Foundation commissioned the American Institutes of Research (AIR) to find out. AIR revisited the themes of equity and education introduced in *How Schools Shortchange Girls*. Using recommendations and insights from the first report, *Gender Gaps: Where Schools Still Fail Our Children* assesses the progress toward equity since 1992, reconceptualizes the problem, and identifies new issues in gender equity.

Profound changes in school demographics and new challenges in American education demand scrutiny in their impact on gender relations and equity. The report examines these conditions, including the rise in technology, a focus on educational standards and related assessments, and the creation of new academic curricula and programs, such as School to Work initiatives. Finally, the new report explores areas of potential equity challenges in the 21st century.

Gender Gaps confirms that public schools *are* making progress toward equitable treatment of boys and girls, although concerns remain. Some of these concerns—such as academic tracking—are long-standing. Others—such as the impact of standards-based teaching—reflect new features of the educational landscape of the late 1990s that have an impact on gender equity.

Over the next five years the Foundation plans to tackle ambitious research questions about gender and education raised in this review. One such question concerns the differential use of classroom technology and teacher professional development. As we develop an information-based economy, more and more 21st-century jobs will require a facility with computer technology. A competitive nation cannot allow girls to write off technology as exclusively male domain. Teachers will need to be prepared to deal with this issue.

Another question concerns girls' and women's "transitions" from school to work, and from work to school. The Foundation plans a new research agenda to examine individual, institutional, and cultural factors that influence moves between the critical spheres of education, family, and career. The preliminary discussion of School-to-Work programs in *Gender Gaps* provides one starting point for such further research.

Finally, the AAUW Educational Foundation will continue to monitor developments in K–12 public school education and educational reform.

Our goal is to ensure equal chances for all public school students to learn, excel, and achieve educationally. As *Gender Gaps* makes clear, the goal of school excellence that drives the standards movement is one and the same goal behind educational equity. The ideas are irreparably linked. Equity without excellence would be a terrible waste of talent. Excellence without equity is a contradiction in terms.

Maggie Ford
President, AAUW Educational Foundation
September 1998

Gender Gaps

◆

GAUGING PROGRESS

◆

American education on the verge of the 21st century looks
considerably different than it did in 1992 when the AAUW
Educational Foundation first published *How Schools Shortchange
Girls*. The student population has grown rapidly: K–12 public
schools enrolled 44.8 million students in the fall of 1995, up
from 41.2 million in 1990.[1] Schools will need to hire more than
two million new teachers by 2006 just to keep pace.

The student population is also more diverse than ever before.
In fall 1986, 70 percent of all students in U.S. public elementary and secondary schools were white; by fall 1995, white
students accounted for 65 percent.[2] More nonwhite teachers
are needed to match the classroom's changing racial, ethnic,
and socioeconomic complexion.

With the new student composition have come new challenges. The Hispanic population, "poised to become the largest
ethnic minority in the United States," has a particularly high
dropout rate from K–12 education: About one in five Hispanic
females leaves school by age 17, a rate higher than that for
any other group of girls.[3] And despite greater student diversity, says Maria Rebledo Monetcel of the Intercultural
Development Research Association, "we continue to prepare
teachers for nonexistent students: middle-class students who
speak English and have plenty of resources at home."[4]

Changes go beyond demographics. Experiments in alternate
forms of education include charter schools (allowed by 29
states in 1997), home schooling (now practiced for at least

500,000 children nationwide), the movement for school choice, and School-to-Work programs that link the classroom to the workplace.

While computer technology is taking instruction beyond tradition-al classroom walls, the physical walls of many aging and poorly financed schools are crumbling. Some districts have sought help from corporate quarters, taking school management into new ter-rain. More broadly, an increased cor-porate presence in school (through Channel One and other commercial-ly sponsored curriculum materials) is blurring the line between educa-tion and marketing. Other social pressures are impinging on schools. Violence is among them. In 1997–98, multiple killings on K–12 school property cost 16 lives.[5]

In the face of these tumultuous changes, educators in the 1990s have not been idle. Across the nation, teachers and school adminis-trators are experimenting with new ways of organizing teaching and learning, through a host of reform efforts designed to raise student achievement. Besides scrutinizing how teachers teach and how stu-dents learn, education reformers have questioned how learning should be provided and measured. By 1998 thirty-eight states had adopted educational standards.[6] At the federal level, the Goals 2000 ini-tiative outlined six national educa-tional goals: readiness to learn, high graduation rates, demonstrated

competencies, science and mathematics achievement, literacy, and
safe and drug-free schools.[7]

Finally, schools have invested
enormous resources—more than
$5 billion in 1997—in equipping
schools with computer technology. A 1998 study notes,
"Technology's stock is flying high
in the nation's schools," and touts
technology as the "missing linch-
pin of school reform," yet its
instructional advantages or benefits have not been proven.[8] The
rush to embrace computer technology has led classes into unfa-
miliar terrain, exciting but potentially dangerous in its capacity to widen the gender and class gap.

. . . continued from previous page

♦ *Girls and women must play a central role in educational reform. The experiences, strengths, and needs of girls from every race and social class must be considered in order to provide excellence and equity for all our nation's students.*

♦ *A critical goal of education reform must be to enable students to deal effectively with the realities of their lives, particularly in areas such as sexuality and health.*

In the field of education research, *How Schools Shortchange Girls* sparked hundreds of new studies on girls in education, ensuring that girls became central to discussions in class-rooms, schools, districts, states, and across the nation. A clear focus has emerged: To move into the 21st century, girls must receive an education that will help them realize their potential, discover new skills, and achieve economic self-sufficiency in the work force. Educators, education task forces, and educa-tional standards committees, singly and together, have heard this message: Girls must not be shortchanged in schools.

But given the awareness and the changes in the last five years, have we made progress in achieving gender equity? Do new approaches to teaching and learning benefit both girls and boys? What gaps still need to be addressed? Have new issues emerged for girls within the changing educational landscape? This report reiterates the goals of the 1992 report, assesses progress, recon-ceptualizes gender equity, and raises new gender equity themes for the next century.

♦ ♦ ♦

New Approaches to Gender and Education Research

Educational equity implies quality education and equal opportunities for all students. Valerie Lee describes equity as "a concern for unequal educational outcomes by social background"—variables such as sex, class, socioeconomic status, race, and ethnicity.[9] Equity differs from equality, which sets up a comparison, generally between two groups. If our concern were *equality*, the critical question would be whether students receive the *same* education.

Equity poses a different question: Do students receive the *right* education to achieve a shared standard of excellence? Although "equity" implies that students' educational performance and outcomes will be the same across groups of students, it does not imply that students need the same things to *achieve* those outcomes. Equity is a difficult and complex concept, particularly in U.S. culture, which thinks more of equality—sameness—than equity.[10] As Ellen Wahl writes, "The idea that same might not be equal is not a well-accepted concept in this society. Eric Jolly often uses the example of two children, one starving and the other overweight. He asks, 'Do you feed them the same diet?'"[11]

Rejecting the Deficit Model

Equitable education, ideally, addresses the needs of both girls and boys, rather than questioning whether each receives the same thing. In practice, though, definitions of equity often have implied an opposition—that is, boys have advantages, and girls do not. This logic views boys as the norm against which girls are measured: Boys are "top performers." Girls need to "catch up." Girls tend to be compared to boys in a limited number of subject areas—those in which they are outperformed by boys. Rather than challenge the unequal distribution of resources in education as an institutional problem, this version of equity proposes that girls must overcome their deficits in comparison to boys.

The "deficit model" of equity sets other limits. The model tends to focus nearly exclusively on what is wrong with girls rather than what is right. This approach leaves little room for the recognition and leveraging of strengths, abundant though they are for girls of all racial and socioeconomic groups. Programs based on the deficit model typically focus on "fixing" girls who fall short of boys, and dispelling myths that "girls can't do science/math/technology." Adherents typically fail to see that boys, having outperformed girls on some subjects, could stand to learn from girls on others—that they might in fact benefit from cultivating some of girls' strengths. To be sure, some deficit model programs have produced positive outcomes for girls, but, crucially, these outcomes focus less on institutions—and institutional changes in how we think about learning or gender relations—and more on changing individual girls.[12]

Probing Intra-Gender Differences

Racial, class, and ethnic differences have further complicated the equity question in education research since 1992. Girls are not a uniform group, nor are their needs singular. Over the past five years, research on girls has moved from an assumption of homogeneity to a focus on "intra-gender" differences—differences among girls.[13] An exploration of differences not only between the undifferentiated populations of "boys and girls" but also among the population of girls by race, ethnicity, or class makes research more complex, but produces a more finely detailed, accurate portrait of students' school identities.

When other social variables are introduced into gender equity research, studies begin to challenge who, precisely, is meant by the term "girls." For example, Carol Gilligan's pathbreaking work on female adolescence in the 1980s noted that girls suffer a drop in self-esteem during their teenage years, slowly losing their voice and becoming less intellectually and socially confident. Yet 1991 research discovered that black girls of the same age do not, in fact, experience the drop in self-esteem that Gilligan observed in the population she studied—predominantly white, upper-class girls attending an elite private school.[14] The observation that adolescent girls lose self-esteem, unless it is modified by race, buries the experiences of African American girls under the general category of "girls."

Research on differences among girls also challenges the idea that Caucasian students always have advantages, and African American and Hispanic students always have secondary deficits because of race. Researchers today increasingly recognize that Caucasians should no more be the model against which African Americans and Hispanics are measured than boys should be the model against which girls are compared. Undoubtedly, a nonwhite girl in American schools often does face both gender and race discrimination. Yet research has documented that African American girls as a population have higher self-esteem, healthier body image, and greater social assertiveness than their white female counterparts, and stronger academic performance by many indicators than their black male counterparts.

Clarifying assumptions about who "girls" are and how schools ideally should operate helps us redefine our notions of educational equity. Instead of comparing girls only to boys, we also compare boys to girls, and compare girls against their own prior performance. Instead of limiting comparisons to areas that emphasize traditional male strengths, we extend the analysis to include girls' strengths. Differences in educational outcome by gender—whether these differences favor boys or girls—belong in the equity research agenda. And instead of presenting girls as a uniform group, we recognize the diversity of girls. It is important to note that, in 1998, researchers are just beginning to collect and examine data by both race and gender, and the scale of such efforts is still quite limited.

Acknowledging Individual Differences

We also recognize that girls and boys *as individuals* are diverse. Clearly, not all girls suffer from fear of math, or conform to stereotypes of feminine behavior, and not all boys judge literacy a female domain. Individual experiences quite often defy statistical norms, as parents, teachers, and students will readily confirm. Furthermore, girls and boys are far more alike in their skills, competencies, and educational outcomes than they are different.

Research on equity and education examines differences in the *aggregate*, between *populations* of girls and *populations* of boys, rather than between individual boys and girls. It asks, in David Tyack's words, "How do schools look when viewed through the lens of gender?"[15] Equity researchers are interested in differences between populations that cannot be explained by chance or by varying individual preferences. These kinds of differences—ones that exist between populations—are the much-discussed "gaps," or uneven outcomes, to which gender equity refers.

The deficits and strengths we identify throughout this report, in our view, do not *innately* belong to girls or boys. Differences between girls and boys, or between and among racial groups or socioeconomic categories, cannot and should not be attributed to biological differences. Girls are not *inherently* more talented in writing, languages, or music. Opportunities and expectations are shaped by social phenomena, notably the idea that there are two genders, with oppositional characteristics. The idea is conveyed as a social expectation, both inside and outside of school, and influences the ways that girls view themselves, as well as how adults view them. Social forces shape the strengths that girls and boys develop, which are then displayed and sometimes reinforced in schools. Regardless of the sources of gender gaps—whether "nature" or "nurture"—schools have a mission to educate all students to levels of competency and to broaden individual opportunities rather than reinforce group stereotypes about student skills and options.

Rethinking the Role of Schools

Advancing the goal of equity requires institutional and systematic change, rather than an emphasis on changing girls or boys to conform better to the educational status quo. School personnel—teachers, coaches, counselors, and administrators—are powerfully situated to challenge stereotypes about what girls and boys can and cannot do. The surest way to reinforce these limiting stereotypes is by failing to act. Limitations on student behavior appear in the uneven interests of girls and boys (evidenced by course taking, for example) and uneven pursuit of career options. When we speak of equity for girls, we refer to several aspects of equity, including: equity in access, equity in resources, and equity in outcomes.[16] Equity, from this perspective, is dependent in many cases on institutional and systematic change in education.

Throughout this report, we contend there is an inherent and crucial link, rather than a conflict, between the achievement of equity goals and the achievement of high academic standards for all students. In many respects, the two movements seek the same objective: educational outcomes that don't vary by gender, race, class, or ethnicity. Standards propose that all students can succeed, no matter how disadvantaged or challenged they are. Similarly, the equity agenda proposes that educational outcomes need not be determined by social background. Indeed, by definition, an inequitable education (one that produces uneven achievement for some groups—for example, girls in science or math) falls short of the standards movement goal of comparable—and high—levels of achievement for all students.

However, the link between equity and rigorous, uniform educational standards has been missed in much of the implementation of education reform. Setting high standards for all students is both a compelling and dangerous goal: In many cases, the goal obscures the needs of historically disadvantaged groups. Hence, the crucial goal of seeing students in public schools achieve to "the same" high standards is not linked to equity concerns—the recognition that particular groups may need different things from their education to achieve the same standards. In this report we consider the potential of standards—*when paired with the equity agenda*—to achieve in reality what it supports in rhetoric: meeting the needs of *all students*.

Organization of the Report

Rather than starting from what needs to be changed, as many traditional gender equity models have done, this report starts with what is known about girls' strengths and achievements.

Chapter 1 surveys and compares girls' and boys' course-taking patterns, noting changes since 1992. Chapter 2 looks at assessments and outcomes—tests and grades—and examines unequal outcomes by gender. Chapter 3 discusses the link between educational equity and the movement toward high standards for all students. After examining standards (as they read on paper), the chapter reviews the degree to which instructional resources such as textbooks, technology, teaching styles, and teacher training have been used, or not used, to advance equity in the classroom. Chapter 4 examines the factors that put students at academic risk, and considers school efforts to lessen students' vulnerability to those risks.

Chapter 5 moves outward from the classroom to consider the larger school context, examining students' participation in extracurricular activities, primarily sports. Chapter 6 examines efforts to correct lopsided job distribution patterns and to inform student decision-making about careers through school counseling, mentoring, and to School-to-Work programs. Chapter 7, "Monitoring Gender Equity in the 21st Century," reviews some measures for charting progress and explores potential gender equity themes for the future.

....

CHAPTER ONE

Course-Taking Patterns

◆

The courses students take in high school and the degree to which they master these subjects affect the choices open to them for years to come. College acceptances, scholarship offers, and employment opportunities can hinge on student course-taking decisions and subsequent performance. Understandably, this area has drawn researchers' attention over the past several years.

Much of this attention has focused on math and science courses, where boys have historically outnumbered and out-performed girls. This gap is a portent of the gender gap in college math and science programs and, later, in well-paying math and science careers. The rapid growth of technology has also fueled concern about girls' computer skills, which generally lag behind boys'. Boys significantly outnumber girls in higher-skill computer courses, while girls tend to cluster in lower-end data entry and word processing classes.

This chapter reviews girls' and boys' uneven participation across the entire curriculum. We review not just girls' much-researched and discussed participation rates in science, mathematics, and computer science, but also boys' participation in English, foreign language, social sciences, and the arts. Examining gender differences among boys and girls, across the curriculum, reflects the goals of educational equity research, which attempts to document different educational outcomes according to factors such as sex, race, or class, regardless of which group these differences favor.

....

As Valerie Lee explains, "reading, writing, social studies, and foreign language are seldom discussed in the [gender equity] venue, although gender differences exist in these areas. ... Why should we examine only curriculum areas where girls are disadvantaged?"[1]

Subject Enrollments

Girls' participation is improving in some academic areas where it previously lagged, particularly in math and science. The number of courses taken in a discipline, however, doesn't tell the whole story; class-by-class comparisons show that girls are still less well represented in some higher-level courses in math, science, and computer science. Boys' participation, meanwhile, is lower in some of the humanities, including English, language, sociology, psychology, and the fine arts.

Girls' enrollments are up in mathematics and science courses, and the difference between girls' and boys' course patterns here appears to be narrowing. Girls still enroll in language arts courses (including foreign languages) with greater frequency than boys. In fact, course-taking patterns, when viewed as a whole, suggest that girls may be getting a broader education than boys by deepening their exposure to math and science and by enrolling in more courses in other subject areas.

Mathematics

A much-discussed gap between girls and boys—average numbers of mathematics courses taken—appears to be diminishing. But gender differences remain in the kinds of courses taken. In an encouraging develop-

---

EMPHASIZING MATH AND SCIENCE

1992 Goal: *Girls must be educated and encouraged to understand that mathematics and the sciences are important and relevant to their lives. Girls must be actively supported in pursuing education and employment in these areas.* (How Schools Shortchange Girls, *page 86*)

Analysis: In 1992 virtually every aspect of mathematics and science education was found to be lacking: Stereotypes of mathematics and science as inappropriate for girls and women were ubiquitous, classroom bias was apparent in these content areas, and women were underrepresented among mathematics and science college majors despite having sufficient background and abilities. The report also found apparent differences in the effectiveness of new science curricula favoring males.

. . . continued

---

ment, more girls are enrolling in algebra, geometry, precalculus, trigonometry, and calculus than in 1990. However, girls are more likely than boys to end their high school math careers with Algebra II.

Both the Council of Chief State School Officers and the 1994 High School Transcript Study found that males and females take comparable numbers of high school mathematics courses.[2] In 1994—the most recent year for which data is available—both groups averaged nearly 3.5 credits of math courses.

Yet an examination of course-by-course enrollment figures for girls and boys reveals remaining gender divisions. A significantly larger proportion of male than female high school graduates took the lowest-level high school mathematics courses (basic mathematics and general mathematics), according to 1994 data from the High School Transcript Study.[3] Girls outnumber boys in algebra and geometry. Roughly equal proportions of girls and boys take precalculus or calculus prior to leaving high school.

In another sign that the overall math gap is shrinking, more girls entered Algebra I, Algebra II, geometry, precalculus, trigonometry, and calculus in 1994 than in 1990. This finding is encouraging in light of research that cites taking Algebra I and geometry early in high school—generally in the ninth and tenth grades—as the major predictor of a student's continuing on to college.[4] Additionally, in 1994, roughly equal numbers of girls and boys took precalculus, trigonometry, and statistics/probability enrollments.[5] (See Table 1.)

Among college-bound girls, enrollment in math courses has increased more over the past decade than it has for college-bound boys, according to ACT, Inc., a nonprofit organization best known for its college admissions testing program. In this population, more females than males now take geometry and second-year algebra. In addition, the proportion of girls taking trigonometry and calculus has increased by 7 and 9 percent

. . . continued from previous page

1998 Reality: Of all the 1992 goals, this one has perhaps seen the most, or at least the most measurable, success. Innumerable programs have debunked myths and stereotypes surrounding girls' involvement in mathematics and science. Girls' test scores and course enrollments have risen perceptibly in these areas, with the exception of computer science. The National Science Foundation in particular has funded a number of promising initiatives. An evaluation of these is in progress.

Table 1
Percentage of 1990 and 1994 High School Graduates Taking Specific Mathematics Courses by Gender

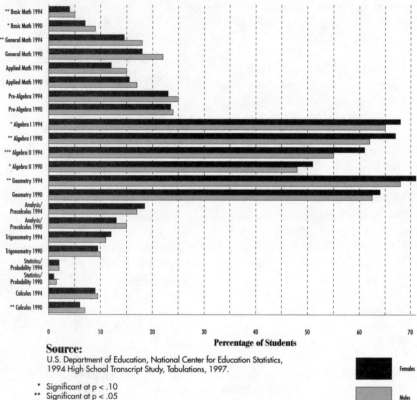

Percentage of Students

Source:
U.S. Department of Education, National Center for Education Statistics,
1994 High School Transcript Study, Tabulations, 1997.

■ Females

□ Males

* Significant at p < .10
** Significant at p < .05
*** Significant at p < .01

respectively since 1987, while the percentage of boys taking trigonometry has held steady and the percentage enrolling in calculus has increased by only 6 percent. Between 1987 and 1997 college-bound girls' enrollment in geometry also increased by 8 percent; in Algebra II it increased by 15 percent. In contrast, college-bound boys' enrollment in those courses rose by 5 and 10 percent.[6]

State-level data collected by the Council of Chief State School Officers indicates that slightly greater percentages of girls enrolled in Algebra II/Integrated Math in 1996 than in 1990. Seven of eighteen states reporting data by gender indicated

GENDER GAPS: WHERE SCHOOLS STILL FAIL OUR CHILDREN

increases, ranging from 1 to 6 percent, from 1990 to 1996. Twelve of the eighteen states reported an increase in girls' enrollments in trigonometry/precalculus (from 2 to 6 percent) over the same time period.[7]

However, girls are significantly more likely than boys to end their high school mathematics careers with Algebra II. Fifty-three percent of girls versus 47 percent of boys end their high school mathematics careers with the completion of this course. Stopping a math education at this level can close the door on future studies, scholarships, and careers.

Science

A greater percentage of female high school graduates took science courses in 1994 than in 1990. Girls are more likely than their male counterparts to take both biology and chemistry. Roughly equal proportions of girls and boys enroll in engineering and geology. Physics, however, remains a largely male domain. While more girls enroll today than in 1990, the gender gap here is sizeable.

CHANGES IN GRADUATION REQUIREMENTS

A high school's graduation requirements and the availability of honors and advanced placement courses provide the context in which students choose which courses to pursue.

Minimum high school graduation requirements in computers, mathematics, and science have risen since 1990. In 1990, 12 states required at least 2.5 credits of mathematics and four states required at least 2.5 credits of science. By 1996, 2.5 or more years of mathematics and science were required in 18 and 11 states respectively.

Students' selection of courses can be influenced by minimum high school graduation requirements. Since all students—girls and boys—must fulfill these minimum requirements, the type of course taken or timing of course enrollment may be a more accurate equity indicator.

Even though male and female high school students take a similar average number of science courses, males are more likely than females to have taken all three of the core science courses—biology, chemistry, and physics—by graduation. Girls' enrollment in physics has been increasing, but a significant gender gap persists. The science education community acknowledges the "physics problem" and has developed interventions to increase girls' participation.[8] Science reforms are more recent than those in mathematics, which may partly explain the lingering disparity between girls' and boys' participation in physics.[9] (See Table 2.)

Table 2
Percentage of 1990 and 1994 High School Graduates Taking Specific Science Courses by Gender

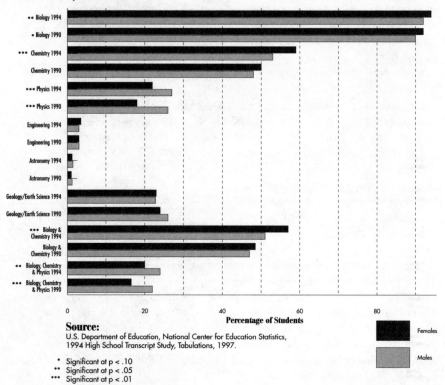

Source:
U.S. Department of Education, National Center for Education Statistics, 1994 High School Transcript Study, Tabulations, 1997.

* Significant at p < .10
** Significant at p < .05
*** Significant at p < .01

■ Females
▨ Males

Computer-Related Studies

Enrollments in higher-skill computer courses show a puzzling drop for both boys and girls, although boys clearly outnumber girls. In comparison, girls tend to cluster in lower-end data entry and word processing classes that lead to less stimulating jobs.

States' lavish investment in computers across K–12 education has visibly transformed the appearance and teaching philosophy of many public schools. Yet, for reasons that are unclear, fewer boys and girls are enrolling in computer science classes that prepare students for careers in computer programming and theory. The enrollment drop is puzzling in light of burgeoning industry needs for technically skilled workers.

Computer applications courses in graphic arts and computer-aided design, while not especially common, attract very few girls. Girls are significantly more likely than boys to enroll in clerical and data entry classes, the 1990s version of typing. (See Table 3.)

Table 3
Percentage of 1990 and 1994 High School Graduates Taking Specific Computer Courses by Gender

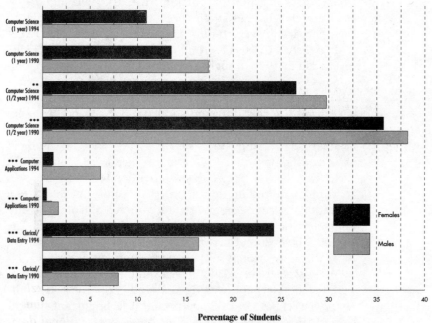

Percentage of Students

Source:
U.S. Department of Education, National Center for Education Statistics, *Vocational Course Taking and Achievement: An Analysis of High of High School Transcripts and 1990 NAEP Assessment Scores* (Washington, DC: 1995).

** Significant at p < .05
*** Significant at p < .01

English

Girls outnumber boys in all English classes except remedial English, earning more credits here than boys.

No advocate of high educational standards and improved U.S. public education questions the need for literacy, reading, writing, and oral communications skills as prerequisites for success in all careers.[10] In the standards movement, literacy denotes not only reading comprehension and traditional courses in English literature, but also spoken language, technological communication, knowledge of written, spoken and visual texts, and knowledge of the processes involved in creating, interpreting, and critiquing such texts.[11]

Despite the centrality of language arts to the criteria of excellent education, boys and girls do not pursue the languages arts in equal proportion. In both 1990 and 1994, female high school graduates were more likely than males to have enrolled in every type of English course except for remedial English.[12] Girls as a group earned more than four credits of English in 1994, a slight rise from 1990. Boys as a population also score lower than girls on verbal skills on most standardized tests.[13]

Crucially, gender differences in language arts performance and course taking rarely are noted in discussions of equity or standards. According to Elisabeth Hayes, "one of the most striking findings" in a 1996 study of gender and literacy, in fact, "was the real lack of serious attention to gender issues in scholarship on reading education."[14] Yet equity means that an educational system does not produce uneven outcomes by any characteristic of social background—in this case, gender. The fact that boys do not perform to girls' level in certain subject areas therefore belongs in the gender equity discussion.

A few studies since 1992 have examined why girls excel in verbal, language, and writing skills, and how their strengths shape the school's overall approach to this important content area of the curriculum. (See Table 4.) A cross-national comparison in 1996 found that gender differences are more apparent for the language arts than for mathematics, and perhaps emerge out of a widespread cultural belief that language arts is a female domain. The perception of literacy, reading, writing, and verbal precocity as feminine characteristics shapes the way schools teach reading: They may cater to girls' interests and strengths, promoting "versions of literacy that appeal more to girls than boys."[15] Girls' acuity with language results in a deeper, more imaginative engagement with the writing process and with reading material. A 1992 study examined student journals of their reading experiences and reactions to a novel taught in school. Researchers discovered that "girls were much more apt to write their internal response as they read a novel than boys, and when the book had two strong main characters, girls made more entries about these characters [and identified them by name] than boys."[16]

Student acceptance of purportedly "natural" male and female strengths has undoubtedly fed the expectation that boys will lag behind in the language arts. When researchers in one study asked students why girls and boys differ in reading

Table 4
Percentage of 1990 and 1994 High School Graduates Taking Specific English Courses by Gender

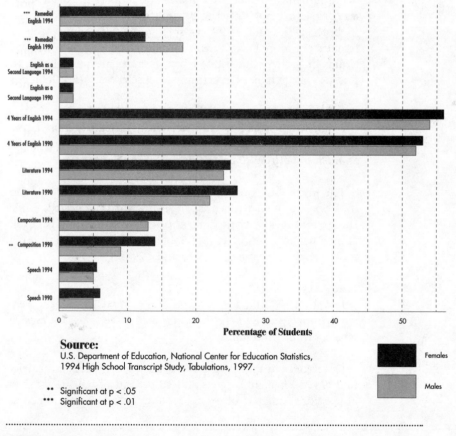

Source:
U.S. Department of Education, National Center for Education Statistics, 1994 High School Transcript Study, Tabulations, 1997.

** Significant at p < .05
*** Significant at p < .01

Females

Males

performance, the largest category of responses was, "It's the way things are."[17] By the time they leave school, students exhibit deeply entrenched ideas of male and female domains of competency. Yet boys and girls do not begin their formal education with these notions. Perceptions of girls as uniquely suited for the language arts appear to intensify after the fourth grade and are most dramatic in the last years of high school.[18]

Social Studies

In the social studies field, encompassing such courses as history, geography, anthropology, economics, sociology, and psychology, more girls than boys tend to enroll in sociology and psychology.

Enrollment differences for males and females in social studies courses are not statistically significant. The one exception, in both 1990 and 1994, is sociology/psychology, where females are more likely to enroll than males. The pattern continues in higher education, where females are more likely to pursue college majors in certain social sciences.[19] (See Table 5.)

Foreign Languages

Female high school graduates were significantly more likely than male high school graduates to have taken French or Spanish in both 1990 and 1994.

The percentages of students, both male and female, who took Spanish increased across the four-year time period, while the percentages of both male and female students who took French declined slightly. (See Table 6.) More girls than boys took French or Spanish in 1990 and 1994.

Fine Arts

In both 1990 and 1994, female high school graduates were significantly more likely than males to have taken courses in music, drama, and dance.

Differences in both years were particularly large in music; in 1994, 44 percent of girls and 28 percent of boys had taken at least one semester of music, including participation in band

Table 5
Percentage of High School Graduates Taking Specific Social Studies Courses in 1990 and 1994 by Gender

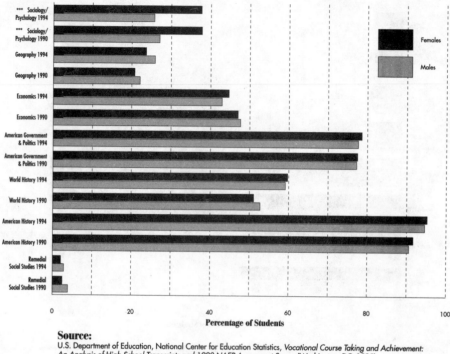

Percentage of Students

Source:
U.S. Department of Education, National Center for Education Statistics, *Vocational Course Taking and Achievement: An Analysis of High School Transcripts and 1990 NAEP Assessment Scores* (Washington, DC: 1995).

*** Significant at p < .01

or orchestra. Males and females enrolled in courses in art or music appreciation at fairly comparable rates in 1990, although relatively few students of either sex had taken courses of this type while in high school. (See Table 7.)

There is some evidence that girls' higher enrollments in fine arts and music may enhance their performance in other subject areas. The National Education Association noted in 1997 that students who took four years of high school art or music classes scored an average 32 points higher on the verbal section of the SAT and an average 23 points higher in math.[20]

◆ ◆ ◆

Table 6
Percentage of 1990 and 1994 High School Graduates Taking Specific Foreign Language Courses by Gender

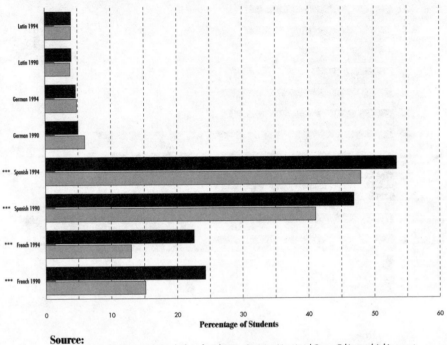

Percentage of Students

Source:
U.S. Department of Education, National Center for Education Statistics, *Vocational Course Taking and Achievement: An Analysis of High School Transcripts and 1990 NAEP Assessment Scores* (Washington, DC: 1995).

*** Significant at p < .01

Females Males

Health and Physical Education

Fewer students are taking physical education now than in 1990, and the dropoff is steeper for girls than boys.

Differences between males and females appear to have increased somewhat between 1990, when 67 percent of females and 70 percent of males had taken a year of physical education, and 1994, when the respective percentages declined to 61 and 67 percent.[21]

Research links physical activity for girls to higher self-esteem, positive body image, and lifelong health. Young females are twice as likely to be inactive as young males.[22]

Table 7
Percentage of 1990 and 1994 High School Graduates Taking Specific Fine Arts Courses by Gender

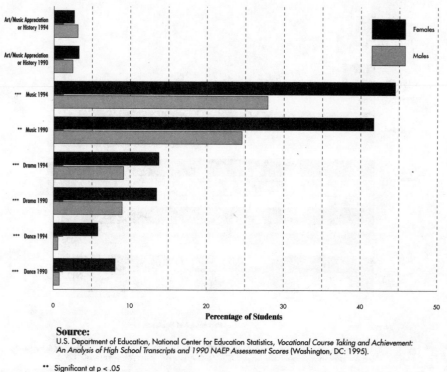

Percentage of Students

Source:
U.S. Department of Education, National Center for Education Statistics, *Vocational Course Taking and Achievement: An Analysis of High School Transcripts and 1990 NAEP Assessment Scores* (Washington, DC: 1995).

** Significant at p < .05
*** Significant at p < .01

Male high school graduates were more likely than females to have taken at least one year of physical education. Although more girls now participate in a wider array of physical activities and sports than ever before, the decline in physical education is troubling, especially given the secondary academic benefits associated with girls' athletic participation.[23] (See Table 8.)

◆ ◆ ◆

Table 8
Percentage of 1990 and 1994 High School Graduates Taking Specific Health and Physical Education Courses by Gender

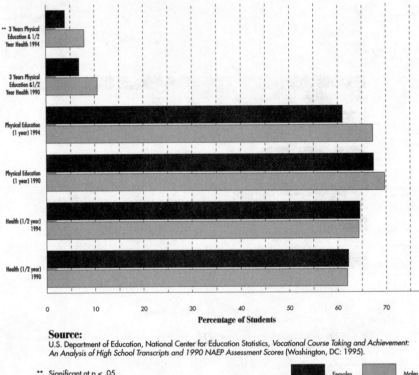

Source:
U.S. Department of Education, National Center for Education Statistics, *Vocational Course Taking and Achievement: An Analysis of High School Transcripts and 1990 NAEP Assessment Scores* (Washington, DC: 1995).

** Significant at p < .05

■ Females   ▨ Males

Remedial and Special Education

....

Girls are likelier than boys to have their abilities overlooked, particularly in math and science. Nonwhite and nonaffluent students—girls and boys—are most likely to be steered to remedial classes.

Schools play a pivotal role in allocating or withholding opportunities to students by identifying them as "regular," "college preparatory," "gifted and talented," or "learning disabled," or otherwise designating their ability level.[24] National data show that school policies of sorting or "tracking" students into lower-level classes result in less actual learning for both boys and girls overall. Maureen Hallinan asserts, "Empirical research provides considerable evidence that the quality and quantity of instruction increases with track level," and that "the higher the track level, the greater the students' academic status, self-esteem, and motivation to learn."[25] Jomills Braddock and Robert Slavin write that "being in the low track in eighth grade slams the gate on any possibility that a student can take the courses leading to college. The gate remained open for equally low-achieving eighth graders who had the good fortune to attend untracked schools."[26]

In theory, tracking might advance gender equity because it groups students according to their academic skills, rather than arbitrary variables such as race, socioeconomic status, or sex. However, some researchers have concluded that ratings of academic talents and skills are mediated by race, gender, and socioeconomic status, among other factors. Recognition of physical disabilities in schools are proportionate across the sexes, but recognition of more subjective disabilities such as learning disorders are not. This suggests that gender expectations bias tracking decisions.[27] Sally Reis and Carolyn Callahan found that male teachers, in particular, tend to stereotype girls and their talents.[28] Such critical judgments of their abilities deter many girls from persevering particularly in mathematics and sciences.[29] Nonwhite and nonaffluent students—girls and boys—are especially likely to have their abilities overlooked.[30]

JENNIFER'S STORY

Despite the ubiquitous nature of informal tracking, teachers and schools often go to great lengths to prove to students that ability grouping does not exist. However, the argument does not fool the students.

"Hello. My name is Jennifer and I am in seventh grade, and I just turned 13 a little while ago. I have a teacher who puts us into groups, and the groups are smart group and dumb group.

"She doesn't say they're smart group and dumb group, but they are the smart group and dumb group. All the smart people are in the smart group, and all the other people are in the dumb group, and I'm always in the dumb group because I always have been in the dumb group."

Source:
Kathleen deMarrais, and Margaret LeCompte, *The Way Schools Work: A Sociological Analysis in Education* (White Plains, N.Y.: Longman Publishers, 1995): 214.

Significantly, placement into "remedial," special education, or lower academic tracks often occurs as students enter school in the fall—a difficult time for many students. Because tracking occurs so early in the school year, teachers and administrators may not have learned enough about individual students to challenge prior gender-stereotyped expectations. The earlier in the year a student is tracked, the more likely the decision is affected by stereotypes of performance and behavior rather than substantive knowledge—acquired only over time—of the student's abilities. Students who experience difficulties in the first few weeks of school often have trouble later with grades, behavior, grade retention, absenteeism, and dropping out of school.[31]

Advanced Placement, Gifted, and Honors Programs

In 1992 enrollments in gifted programs favored girls. No new data contradict this finding.[32] However, girls drop out of high school gifted tracks at a faster rate than boys.

Participation in top-level high school courses and in gifted and honors programs indicate, in large part, how teachers, parents, and students themselves perceive their academic abilities and interests. Participation in these courses also powerfully predicts enrollment in higher education.

Most schools identify children for gifted and talented programs at around third grade, on the basis of teacher recommendations and standardized tests.[33] Educators and administrators generally identify girls for gifted programs at equal or greater numbers than boys, yet students are identified for different kinds of programs, according to gender expectations. Schools do not identify girls for their mathematics and science talents in the same proportions as boys, who, likewise, are not identified for their English, language, or arts abilities in the same proportions as girls.[34]

Furthermore, girls are not retained in high-level gifted tracks to the same extent as boys. Despite the early identification of special talent in girls, Carolyn Read found that there is an abrupt reversal of this pattern around the tenth grade.[35]

Something leads many girls not to enroll or to drop out of gifted and talented programs early in high school; others are not identified for these programs. What happens in middle school and early high school to discourage girls' identification with and participation in gifted programs? Read hypothesizes that, during elementary school, educators identify more girls for gifted and talented programs because girls are more likely to meet sex-role expectations.[36] However, as girls reach adolescence, their focus often shifts from being the "good girl" in school to fitting in with peer groups. For girls, fitting in often involves playing dumb, hiding their intelligence, and being quiet.

Sally Reis and M. Katherine Gavin also observed that although teachers in general did not engage in sex-role stereotyping, they did stereotype their best students in the area of mathematics, attributing characteristics such as volunteering answers, enjoying mathematics, and working independently to males.[37] Teachers rated females higher than males on the effort they put into schoolwork and on the quality of their work; however, teachers gave boys and girls the same grades, despite girls' higher ratings on effort and quality of work.[38] Perhaps this occurs because, as Pat Ross maintains, U.S. culture often equates higher expenditure of effort with lower ability.[39]

If educators and peers cast gifted white girls as quiet, good students, they sometimes cast gifted, academically successful black girls as troublemakers rather than as outspoken, independent leaders of tomorrow.[40] Signithia Fordham found "the most salient characteristic of the academically successful [black] females...is a deliberate silence, a controlled response to their evolving, ambiguous status as academically successful students."[41] Research on educational reform and gender has found that school response to girls' behavior plays a crucial role in recasting potentially "unfeminine" traits such as intellectual aggressiveness into positive and encouraged behavior. For example, one study notes, "girls who speak out may be treated as leaders or renegades," depending in some measure on the school's approach to the behaviors.[42]

◆ ◆ ◆

AP and Honors Enrollment

....

Girls' *AP and honors course enrollments are comparable to or greater than those of boys, except in physics. In AP and honors calculus and chemistry, girls' course enrollments improved relative to boys' from 1990 to 1994.*

Advanced placement (AP) and honors courses are generally the highest-level courses high schools offer. Both kinds of courses are taught at an accelerated pace. Honors courses offer students a deeper understanding of the subject matter and challenge them to produce a higher quality of work. AP courses cover material at college level and can earn college credit for students who score 3 or higher on a 5-point voluntary course-end exam.

In 1997, 58 percent of all public high schools offered AP courses. Today, roughly the same percentage of males and females enroll in AP or honors courses in Western civilization, calculus, or chemistry—an improvement over 1990. Overall, girls' enrollments in AP or honors courses are comparable to those of males across all subjects except for AP physics. Girls are significantly more likely than males to enroll in AP or honors courses in English, foreign language, and biology. Except in foreign languages, girls' and boys' participation in AP or honors courses increased between 1990 and 1994.[43] From 1983 to 1993 there was a substantial increase (from 37 to 43 percent) in the proportion of female AP test takers in math and natural science subject areas.[44] (See Table 9.) For a discussion of AP test-taking patterns, see Chapter 2.

....

Table 9
AP Course Taking by Gender, Subject, Year

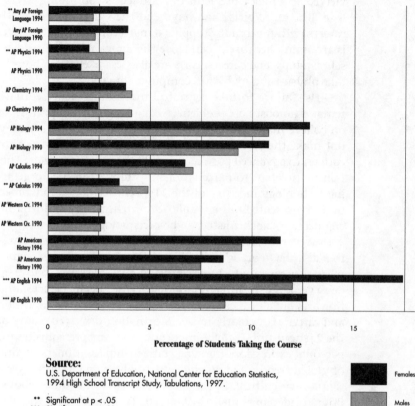

Percentage of Students Taking the Course

Source:
U.S. Department of Education, National Center for Education Statistics,
1994 High School Transcript Study, Tabulations, 1997.

** Significant at p < .05
*** Significant at p < .01

█ Females
▓ Males

Summary

After lagging for years, girls' high school course enrollment patterns are beginning to look more like boys'—an encouraging sign because course selections can open or close future opportunities to students. But progress is not uniform.

In terms of *numbers* of courses taken, girls are closing the much-discussed gap in math and science. But important differences still rest in the specific courses taken. For example, more girls are taking Algebra 1 and geometry today than in

1990. The increase in girls' enrollments is welcome news: Taking Algebra I and geometry by the ninth and tenth grade is viewed as a major predictor of a student's continuing to college. But more girls than boys end their high school math careers with Algebra II. Stopping a math education at this level is troubling because it can close the door on future studies, scholarships, and careers. Girls are also less likely than boys to take physics and high-level computer courses.

Girls' failure to take more top math and science courses remains an obstinate problem, with a long-term impact. Data on college majors and degrees earned indicate that girls may not make the transition from high school math and science courses to advanced postsecondary courses in these fields. This failure threatens to make women bystanders in the burgeoning technology industry of the 21st century and keep women underrepresented in high-salaried, intellectually challenging engineering, biochemistry, and biotechnology careers.

However, to review girls' enrollments in the sciences only is to subscribe to an arbitrary hierarchy of subject areas, and to relegate areas in which girls excel to a lesser status than they deserve. English, foreign languages, the social sciences, and fine arts are all educational prerequisites for higher education and career, particularly in the information-driven economy of the 21st century. Equally important, they are prerequisites for personal expression, informed citizenship, an understanding of global trends, and an ability to analyze and interpret contemporary culture. In these courses, girls outnumber boys. Boys' underenrollment in English, languages, and the arts warrants attention if public schools aspire to achieve high standards for all students.

Schools' practice of tracking students—formally or informally—affects girls' and boys' course-taking patterns differently. Girls are more likely than boys to have their abilities overlooked in math and science—a pattern that limits their future opportunities. On the other hand, girls are also more likely than boys to be identified at a young age for gifted programs. However, girls fall off this gifted track at a higher rate than boys, particularly once they reach high school. There, peer pressure tells many girls to hide their intelligence and be quiet.

The message is received differently by black and white girls, say some researchers. White girls are rewarded for fitting in, for meeting expectations of being the "good girl" in school. Those black girls who are outspoken and independent often find themselves cast as troublemakers rather than leaders. They may pay more of a social price for conforming to expectations of silence.

Roughly the same percentage of boys and girls enroll in the most challenging high school courses: AP and honors courses. Girls' and boys' enrollment in specific AP or honors courses reflects subject enrollment patterns elsewhere: Girls are more likely than boys to enroll in English, foreign language, and biology. Boys are more likely to enroll in physics.

Recommendations

In light of improving participation rates overall for girls in math and science, these recommendations focus on the types and timing of courses boys and girls take.

- In developing curriculum standards, states should make rigorous courses of Algebra I and geometry mandatory for all students, as the gatekeeper classes for college admissions and for advanced study in math, science, engineering, and computer science.
- Schools and school districts should concentrate on increasing the percentage of girls who take the trio of core science courses: physics, biology, and chemistry. In this trio, physics shows the most obstinate gender gap.
- Teachers and counselors should encourage talented girls to take math and science classes at the challenging AP or honors level.
- Educators need to develop interventions at the classroom, school, district, or state level to equalize enrollments in computer science technology. Girls are dramatically underrepresented in regular and AP computer science courses, with the exception of word processing, the 1990s version of typing. This has ramifications beyond the classroom. There already is a shortage of talent to fill high-skill, well-paying jobs in the field.
- Educators should develop curriculum and other incentives to encourage more boys to enroll in fine arts, foreign lan-

guages, advanced English electives, and AP languages and humanities courses. Areas such as these where boys under-enroll or underperform girls are relevant to the equity agenda. Educators should ask: Why do these courses attract fewer boys? Are there curricular changes that might encourage their engagement in these crucial areas of the curriculum?

- States and schools should reassess tracking policies not only in light of racial and class equity concerns, but also in light of gender equity. Currently, educators identify more girls than boys for gifted programs in the elementary years, yet girls are not retained in high-level tracks to the same extent as boys once they reach middle school.
- State and federal data on participation in gifted and special education programs should be disaggregated by sex.

CHAPTER TWO

THE ASSESSMENT PUZZLE

◆

To scholarship committees and college admissions officers, perhaps the only factor more important than the courses students take is how well they perform in them. This chapter examines girls' and boys' performance, including their course grades and scores on standardized tests. For reasons that are not entirely clear, girls consistently earn better grades than boys, but score lower on some standardized tests.

High-stakes tests, with heightened effects on students' lives, reflect a gender gap that is absent in tests given to a more general population. College admissions tests are often considered to underpredict girls' performance in college.

Other tests that are highly selective and competitive likewise tend to magnify gender differences. The advanced placement (AP) test is perhaps the best example. Girls take AP tests in greater numbers than boys overall, and in all subject areas except math, science, and computers, but earn fewer scores of 3 or higher needed to receive college credit. Research notes that the tests rely heavily on multiple-choice questions, where boys seems to have an advantage. Beyond that, however, reasons for the discrepancy in girls' and boys' scores are unclear.

Carole Hollenshead has observed that girls "underperform" boys only on standardized tests, an insight that raises questions about the relationship between standardized tests, in-school performance, and other forms of assessment, including grades.[1] Further, the observation begs the question: If boys test better than girls because they have a better mastery of the material, why don't their grades reflect this?

Efforts continue to revise tests to reduce outcome discrepancies. "In the ideal world," says Jonathan A. Supovitz, "knowing a student's [background] characteristics [such as class, race or gender] would contribute nothing to predicting that student's ... performance" or course-taking history. In other words, according to Supovitz, in an unbiased situation, there would be no "statistical relationship" between course-taking patterns or test performance and gender.[2]

Grades and Assessments

Girls earn equal or higher grades than boys in all subjects throughout their schooling. Girls of all ages, races, and ethnicities also outperformed or were equal performers with boys on the most recent National Assessment of Educational Progress (NAEP) assessments of reading and writing.

Grades are the principal measures used to assess students' mastery of course materials throughout their schooling. Grades are perhaps the most accurate and inclusive measure of performance, as they judge students against the curriculum, and can recognize such important variables as effort, reasoning, and creativity. Marcia Linn and Cathy Kessel argue that grades are the most accurate reflection of whether students have gained applicable, practical skills.[3]

National data indicate that girls consistently earn either equivalent or higher grades than boys in all subjects at all points in their academic careers.[4]

Other measures of student achievement include the National Assessment of Educational Progress, a nationally representative, though voluntary, exam of student knowledge in specific subject areas, administered to a sample of students in the fourth, eighth, and twelfth grades. On the most recent NAEP tests, girls of all ages, races, and ethnic backgrounds matched or surpassed boys' scores in reading and writing.[5] The significant differences favoring boys were in twelfth-grade history, fourth-grade mathematics, twelfth-grade science, and all grade levels of the geography assessments.

Patterns

Scores on standardized tests such as NAEP reinforce traditional beliefs about girls' and boys' areas of relative strength. The highest standardized test scores in reading and writing are earned by girls. Boys earn the highest scores in history, geography, mathematics, and science.

On standardized tests such as NAEP, differences in the proportion of males and females receiving the highest scores favor girls for reading and writing, and boys for history, geography, mathematics, and science. (See Tables 10a, 10b, and 10c.) Beginning in fourth grade, larger proportions of girls than boys receive the highest scores on the NAEP reading and writing assessments. In mathematics and science, a larger proportion of boys receive the top NAEP scores. The gender gap increases in the later grades.

Similarly, the Third International Mathematics and Science Study (TIMSS), an achievement test given to half a million fourth, eighth, and twelfth-grade students in 41 nations in 1995-96, reveals that a gender gap in these fields increases with age. For most countries, including the United States, TIMSS finds small or essentially nonexistent gender differences in mathematics achievement at the fourth-grade level. Gender differences in science were also relatively small at this level. By eighth grade, gender differences in mathematics were still minimal, but gender differences in science were pervasive for most countries.[6]

The TIMSS analysis of twelfth-grade students, released in February 1998, showed males had a significantly higher average achievement than females in mathematics and science literacy in all countries except South Africa. The gender gap in the United States, in fact, was less extreme than that in other countries, perhaps because of the concerted attention to gender equity in math/science education over the last decade. In the United States there were no significant gender differences in mathematics literacy, the most general component of the TIMSS battery of surveys. In contrast, significant gender gaps

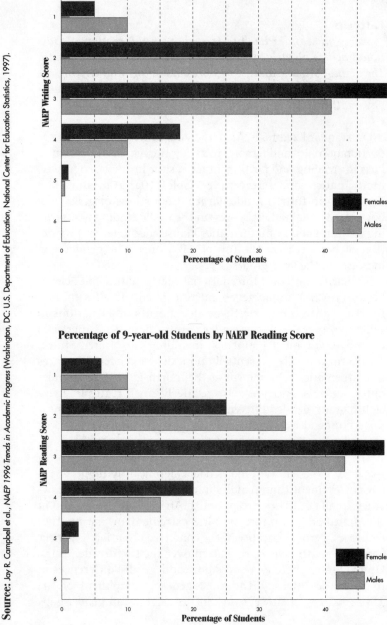

Percentage of 9-year-old Students by NAEP Writing Score

NAEP Writing Score

Percentage of Students

Females

Males

Percentage of 9-year-old Students by NAEP Reading Score

NAEP Reading Score

Percentage of Students

Females

Males

Table 10a Distribution of 1994 and 1996 NAEP Scores by Gender and Subject Area for 9-Year-Olds

1 = Below 150 2 = 150-199 3 = 200-249 4 = 250-299 5 = 300-349 6 = Above 349

Source: Jay R. Campbell et al., *NAEP 1996 Trends in Academic Progress* (Washington, DC: U.S. Department of Education, National Center for Education Statistics, 1997).

Percentage of 9-year-old Students by NAEP Math Score

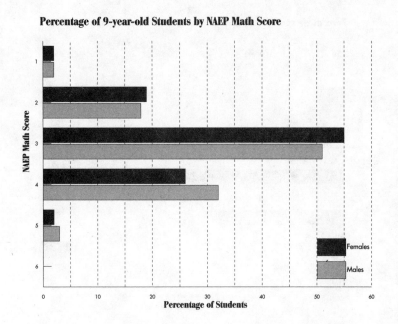

Percentage of 9-year-old Students by NAEP Science Score

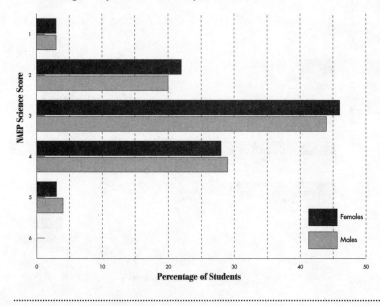

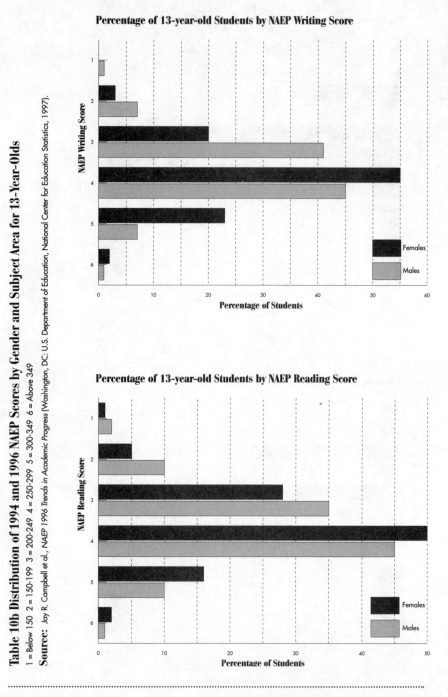

Percentage of 13-year-old Students by NAEP Writing Score

NAEP Writing Score

Percentage of Students

Females

Males

Percentage of 13-year-old Students by NAEP Reading Score

NAEP Reading Score

Percentage of Students

Females

Males

Table 10b Distribution of 1994 and 1996 NAEP Scores by Gender and Subject Area for 13-Year-Olds

1 = Below 150 2 = 150-199 3 = 200-249 4 = 250-299 5 = 300-349 6 = Above 349

Source: Joy R. Campbell et al., *NAEP 1996 Trends in Academic Progress* (Washington, DC: U.S. Department of Education, National Center for Education Statistics, 1997).

GENDER GAPS: WHERE SCHOOLS STILL FAIL OUR CHILDREN

Percentage of 13-year-old Students by NAEP Math Score

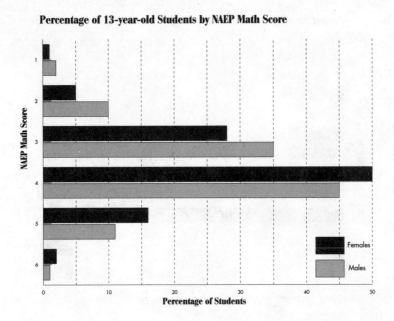

Percentage of 13-year-old Students by NAEP Science Score

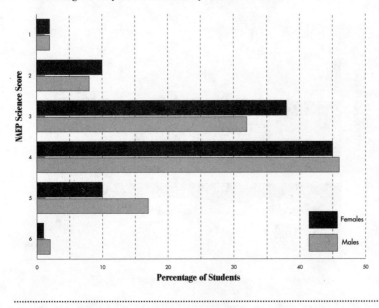

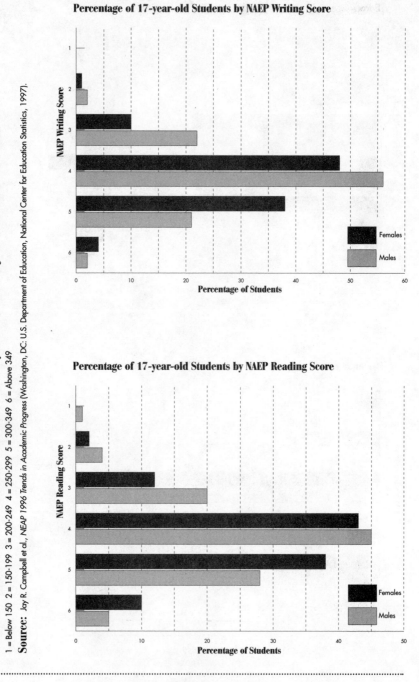

Table 10c Distribution of 1994 and 1996 NAEP Scores by Gender and Subject Area for 17-Year-Olds

1 = Below 150 2 = 150-199 3 = 200-249 4 = 250-299 5 = 300-349 6 = Above 349

Source: Jay R. Campbell et al., *NEAP 1996 Trends in Academic Progress* (Washington, DC: U.S. Department of Education, National Center for Education Statistics, 1997).

Percentage of 17-year-old Students by NAEP Writing Score

NAEP Writing Score

Females

Males

Percentage of Students

Percentage of 17-year-old Students by NAEP Reading Score

NAEP Reading Score

Females

Males

Percentage of Students

Percentage of 17-year-old Students by NAEP Math Score

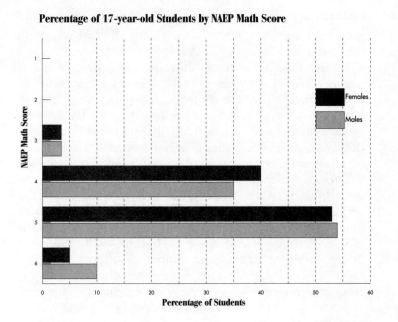

Percentage of 17-year-old Students by NAEP Science Score

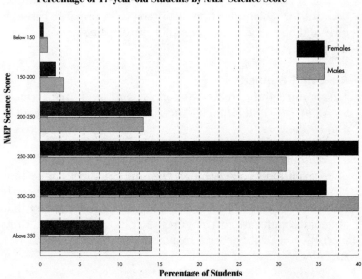

were noted in the "special," more advanced mathematics survey, which measures achievement among students who have taken advanced mathematics classes.

The development of gender differences in mathematics and science achievement paces the decline in the nation's overall international rating: The United States was above average in math/science performance at the fourth-grade level (when gender differences are nonexistent), average in performance at the eighth-grade level (when gender differences, at least in science, become more pronounced) and substantially below the international average in math and science performance by the twelfth grade (when gender differences were marked in the United States and internationally). Raising overall United States performance on math and science—achieving the sought-after high standards for all students—will require fulfilling the equity agenda and combating differences in performance or educational outcome by race, class or, as in this case, gender. Outcome disparities between specific groups of American students—for example, boys and girls—will tend to "drag down" a nation's overall performance in international comparisons.[7]

Subtests of TIMSS and other standardized tests also warrant further examination for gender differences. Research needs to establish whether one or more subsections of the test might account for a disproportionate difference in response between girls and boys and therefore might distort the size of the gender gap on the overall test.

Race and Ethnicity
New data that break down girls' and boys' achievement scores by race and ethnicity show hidden subgroup strengths and weaknesses.

Examining the achievement gap between "girls" and "boys" only—as if these were homogeneous groups—hides important differences under the guise of uniformity. Because white girls outnumber those of other racial and ethnic groups, data that are not disaggregated by race mask some girls' strengths. Only recently have data become available that break down differences by race as well as gender.

Examination of the same data by both race and gender illuminates intra-gender differences. In fourth grade, Hispanic girls score higher than Hispanic boys in reading and history; by the eighth grade, they score higher in mathematics and reading; and by the twelfth grade, they score higher than Hispanic boys in science as well as reading. Similarly, black girls demonstrate academic strengths at every assessment point. In fourth grade, they outpace black male classmates in science, reading, geography, and history. In eighth grade, they retain an advantage over black male classmates in science, reading, and history. In the twelfth grade, they score equally with black boys in mathematics, and retain an advantage in reading. The achievement gap between white girls and white boys is smaller at all assessment points. In the fourth grade, white girls score higher in reading; in the eighth grade, they add a slight advantage in mathematics. By twelfth grade, they hold an advantage in reading only.[8] (See Table 11.)

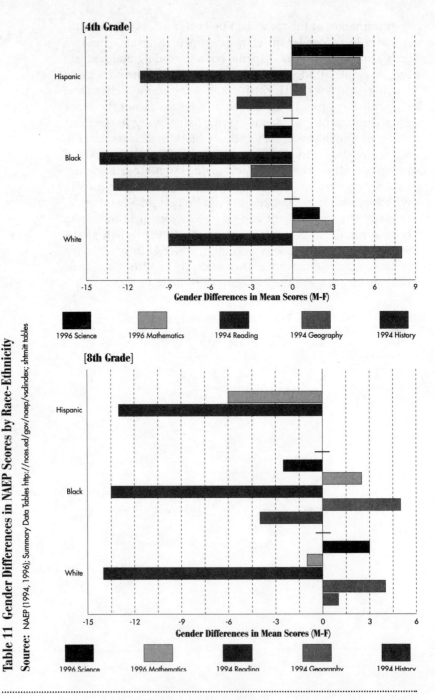

Table 11 Gender Differences in NAEP Scores by Race-Ethnicity

Source: NAEP (1994, 1996); Summary Data Tables http://nces.ed/gov/naep/vsdindex; shmitt tables

[4th Grade]

Gender Differences in Mean Scores (M-F)

-15   -12   -9   -6   -3   0   3   6   9

| 1996 Science | 1996 Mathematics | 1994 Reading | 1994 Geography | 1994 History |

[8th Grade]

Gender Differences in Mean Scores (M-F)

-15   -12   -9   -6   -3   0   3   6

| 1996 Science | 1996 Mathematics | 1994 Reading | 1994 Geography | 1994 History |

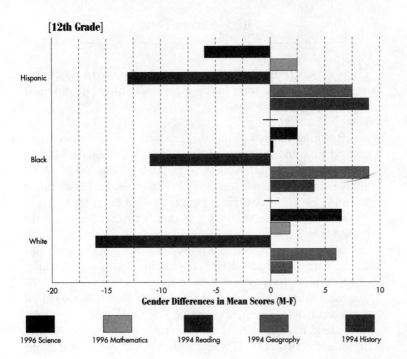

[12th Grade]

Gender Differences in Mean Scores (M-F)

1996 Science   1996 Mathematics   1994 Reading   1994 Geography   1994 History

High-Stakes Tests

High-stakes tests, with disproportionate power to affect students' lives, are the tests that most dramatically reflect gender differences in performance.

Gifted and talented programs, scholarship committees, college admissions offices, and the National Collegiate Athletic Association use high-stakes tests such as the Preliminary Scholastic Assessment Test (PSAT), the Scholastic Assessment Test (SAT), and the American College Testing Program (ACT) to make crucial decisions about a student's future. Scores on the PSAT, taken by students nationwide, usually in the tenth and eleventh grades, determine who will receive 7,400 prestigious and lucrative National Merit Scholarships. SAT and ACT scores often decide college acceptances. Other selective and competitive tests, such as the Advanced Placement (AP) test, also merit extra scrutiny. Research shows that boys and girls, as populations, tend to demonstrate unique strengths in particular test designs, or constructs. For example, multiple-choice sections on exams may favor boys or young men, whereas free-response essay sections may favor young women. Free-response sections, in contrast, that involve mechanical drawing or object rotation tend to favor boys rather than girls. Because specific test constructs may advantage one group of students over another, tests that include multiple answer forms—a combination of essay and multiple choice, for example—may reflect more accurately a student's ability than a test comprised exclusively of free-response or multiple-choice questions.

However, high stakes tests magnify the gender gap in performance.[9] Theresa Anne Cleary concluded, after an extensive 1992 review of 702 data sets from 12 test batteries, that although distributions of female and male test scores generally are more similar than they are different, particularly among a general population, women score lower on more complex and highly selective tests, such as the SAT and AP exams. This gender gap occurs only at the upper percentile levels (among the highest scorers) of the test-taking population and increases with age. Cleary concluded that those who are concerned with the education of young women need to develop programs that will enable them to perform better on more complex tests.[10]

Indeed, although the distribution of SAT-verbal scores was more equitable in 1997, inequities at the tails—the extreme ends—of the SAT-mathematics distribution have not changed substantially since the early 1990s. If, for instance, a scholarship required a minimum SAT-mathematics score of 600, 30 percent of males and 19 percent of females who took the 1997 test would be eligible.

The AP Paradox

Girls take AP tests in greater numbers than boys, but earn lower scores, even in areas of historic strength, such as English. More girls than boys take AP tests in English, social studies, and geography. More boys take the tests in math, science, and computers.

Boys and girls presumably share the same motives for taking AP courses: an eagerness to be challenged by the most demanding courses a school has to offer, and the chance to earn college credit by scoring a 3 or higher on an AP subject exam. Nonetheless, although girls take AP tests in greater numbers overall, and in all subject areas except math, science, and computers, they earn fewer scores of 3 or higher. (See Tables 12 and 13.)

Why girls score lower than boys, on average, across all AP test subject areas—even those in which they otherwise excel—has been the subject of recent research.

The AP examination is arguably the most selective, rigorous, and complex test among those offered to high school students; it is keyed to a specific curriculum followed in AP courses, and includes both multiple-choice and free-response sections. An insight by Cleary applies to the AP exam: The magnitude of the gender gap in scores increases, to male advantage, as the complexity and competitiveness of the test increases. A 1997 study of gender and fair assessment confirms the correlation between test complexity and the more extreme—and surprising—gender gaps consistently evident in AP scores. The research further observed a "gender balance" effect: If a "group is selected [to take a test] in a way that overrepresents females [that is, more girls than boys take the AP

Table 12
Number of AP Examinations Taken Per 1,000 11th and 12th Grade Students by Subject Area and Gender

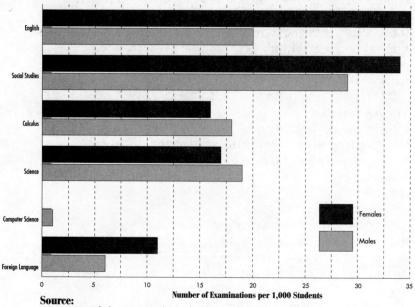

Number of Examinations per 1,000 Students

Source:
U.S. Department of Education, National Center for Education Statistics,
1994 High School Transcript Study, Tabulations, 1997.

Table 13
Proportion of 1995 AP Examinations with Scores of 3 or Higher by Gender

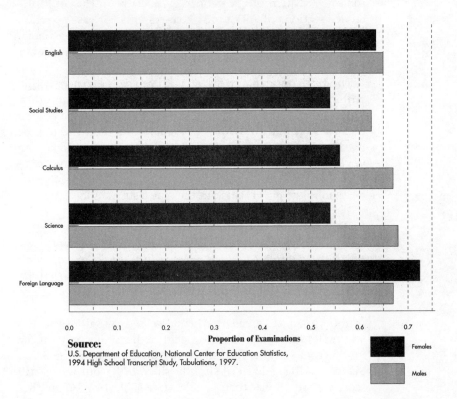

Proportion of Examinations

Source:
U.S. Department of Education, National Center for Education Statistics,
1994 High School Transcript Study, Tabulations, 1997.

English exam], then the ... difference [in scores] will tend to move in a direction favoring the other gender [in this case, males]."[11] Much of the gender gap occurs in the multiple-choice sections of AP exams. Free-response or essay-section scores showed "little gender difference," while multiple-choice scores showed a fairly substantial gap, consistently in favor of boys.

The 1997 research also investigated gender differences within ethnic and racial groups on 1993 AP exams. Although they found more difference between the sexes than they did among racial and ethnic groups, there were two notable exceptions: Black girls were far more likely to take AP examinations than were black boys by a factor of almost two to one. And Asian American girls, relative to boys in their group, did slightly better than white girls on each of the nine tests examined.[12]

PSAT, SAT, and ACT Scores

On the PSAT exam, the 1997 addition of a writing skills section boosted girls' scores and narrowed the gender gap in scores favoring boys. On the SAT and ACT exams, girls as a whole do better than boys only on the ACT verbal section.

In both subject areas (mathematics and verbal) of the SAT and ACT, girls as a whole score higher than boys only on the ACT-verbal section.[13] Mean gender differences on the SAT-I Verbal Test have declined slightly since 1990, but males still score slightly higher than females. (See Table 14.) SAT mathematics test scores have risen for males and females, but the gender difference has not decreased.[14] Males also scored higher than females on the mathematics and scientific reasoning sections of the ACT.[15] Gender differences on the SAT-verbal test favor black girls and girls who did not report their ethnicity. Males of all racial and ethnic backgrounds scored higher than females on the SAT-mathematics test. (See Table 15.)

The addition of a writing-skills assessment section to the PSAT in 1997, however, has narrowed the gap in scores between the sexes. Girls scored an average of 49.8 points on the writing section, 0.8 higher than boys. Although a gap in math scores persists, a "dramatic" change has occurred in the overall scores: Girls' overall score is just 2.7 points lower than that of boys. The previous year's gap was 4.5 points.

Table 14
Mean SAT-Verbal and SAT-Mathematics Scores by Gender, 1990–97

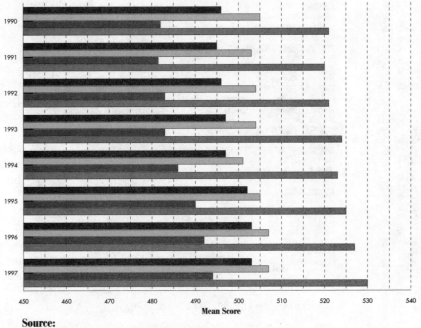

Mean Score

Source:
College Bound Seniors: A Profile of SAT Program Test Takers
(New York: College Entrance Examination Board and Educational Testing Service, 1997)

 Verbal Score–Females

Verbal Score–Males

 Mathematics Score–Females

 Mathematics Score–Males

Table 15 Distribution of 1990 and 1997 SAT-Verbal and SAT-Mathematics Scores by Gender

1 = 200-240 2 = 250-290 3 = 300-340 4 = 350-390 5 = 400-440 6 = 450-490 7 = 500-540 8 = 550-590 9 = 600-640 10 = 650-690 11 = 700-740 12 = 750-800

Source: *College Bound Seniors: A Profile of SAT Program Test Takers* (New York: College Entrance Examination Board and Educational Testing Service, 1997) significant at p<.10

Gender Differences in 1990 SAT-I Verbal Scores

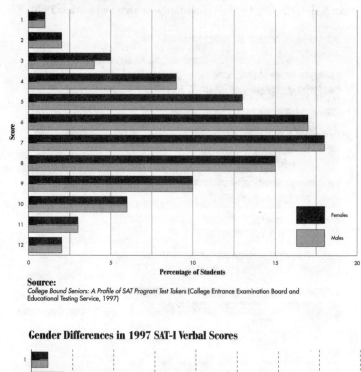

Source:
College Bound Seniors: A Profile of SAT Program Test Takers (College Entrance Examination Board and Educational Testing Service, 1997)

Gender Differences in 1997 SAT-I Verbal Scores

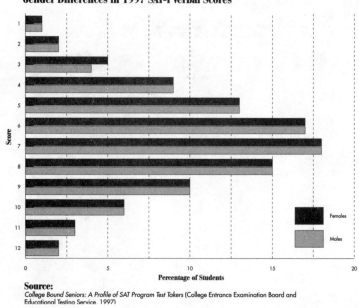

Source:
College Bound Seniors: A Profile of SAT Program Test Takers (College Entrance Examination Board and Educational Testing Service, 1997)

Gender Differences in 1990 SAT-I Math Scores

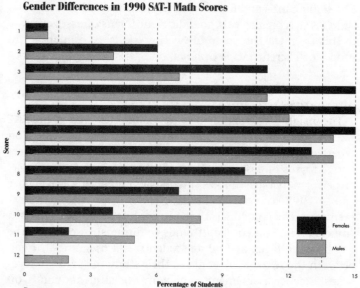

Source:
College Bound Seniors: A Profile of SAT Program Test Takers (College Entrance Examination Board and Educational Testing Service, 1997)

Gender Differences in 1997 SAT-I Math Scores

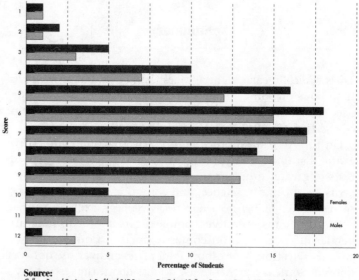

Source:
College Bound Seniors: A Profile of SAT Program Test Takers (College Entrance Examination Board and Educational Testing Service, 1997)

The significant—and fairly sudden—shift toward greater parity in PSAT scores reveals how different forms of assessment—in this case, the inclusion of writing-skills assessment—can produce different views of boys' and girls' academic competencies.[16]

Alternative Assessments

The insight—corroborated somewhat by the change in PSAT scores—that "what you see" on assessments "depends on where you look" has stimulated research into whether alternative forms of assessment—student portfolios, for example, or performance-based assessments—would shrink the gender gap. A 1997 study of Rochester, New York's portfolio assessment system concludes that alternative assessment has a "mixed effect" on equity: It tends to diminish somewhat the gap between black and white students as it magnifies the gap between the sexes. Klein et al., in their study of "performance-based" science assessment (which affords students hands-on opportunities to demonstrate their skills), found that not only did the alternative assessment demonstrate little effect on gender differences in scores, it did not affect racial/ethnic differences either.[17]

Summary

Girls typically earn higher grades than boys, but score lower than boys on some standardized tests and high-stakes tests, used to determine scholarship eligibility and college acceptance or rejection. The SAT and ACT exams are cases in point.

On the AP test, another highly selective and competitive exam, a still more disturbing pattern emerges: Girls take AP tests in greater numbers overall than boys and in all subject areas except math, science, and computers, but earn fewer scores of 3 or higher needed to receive college credit.

Why the most selective, complex tests appear to magnify gender differences in outcomes is unclear. Could students' course selection be responsible? The answer is not yet known. Some researchers raise doubts about the tests' heavy reliance on multiple-choice questions, where boys appear to have an advantage. Both boys and girls appear to be disadvantaged by particular methods of assessment; hence assessment methods must vary to reflect accurately skills and competencies.

Says Jonathan Supovitz, "Of course standardized tests are biased. But it is not just standardized tests—any single testing method is biased because it applies just one approach to getting at student knowledge and achievement. Any single testing method has its own particular set of blinders. Since the bias in testing is intrinsic in the form of assessment used, we cannot eliminate this problem simply by changing the question asked. Rather, we must ask the questions in many different ways."[18]

Efforts to reduce the gap between girls' and boys' scores on some high-stakes tests have proven at least partly successful. The addition of a writing-skills assessment section to the PSAT in 1997 brought about a dramatic change in overall scores. With the addition of the new section, where girls scored an average 0.8 points higher than boys, girls' overall score is just 2.7 points behind boys', down from 4.5 points a year ago. The greater parity in scores shows how varying the forms of assessment can produce different views of boys' and girls' academic competencies.

In addition to examining differential results on portions of high-stakes tests, we must also ask why boys' grades are typically and consistently lower than girls' in all subject areas. High-stakes tests are, in fact, the sole arena in which girls do not perform as well as a group.

Recommendations

....

* Schools need to determine why girls are not taking AP examinations in math, science, and computer science in the same proportion as boys who take the classes. Districts should consider, as some already have, making the AP exam mandatory for all students enrolled in the classes. The exam, keyed to a challenging curriculum, can boost girls' willingness to take risks and to develop confidence with high-level mathematics and science work.

- Districts and states need to invest in the $75 AP exam fee for low-income students.
- The SAT should follow the lead of the PSAT and include a writing component to capture more accurately a student's competencies with basic academic skills.
- Colleges and universities should continue to use a broad range of material to assess student admissions and scholarship eligibility.
- Researchers should continue to examine the relationship between girls' and boys' test scores and grades. Future research should investigate which assessment practices best communicate both group and individual mastery of the curriculum.
- Researchers should continue to explore test score and grade relationships broken down by sex, race, and ethnicity. This can provide important data to develop appropriate equity responses based on individual differences.

CHAPTER THREE

MISSING THE POINT ON STANDARDS

◆

In 1992 some readers criticized the gender equity focus of *How Schools Shortchange Girls*, and the focus on girls as a special group, when reform seemed imperative for all students. Why focus on girls, critics argued, when all students in public schools are underperforming and in need of help? In many respects, however, equity in educational outcomes and the achievement of high standards are two dimensions of the same goal. In fact, the achievement of equity—the erasure of differences in educational quality and outcome by social factors such as race, class, or in this case, gender—is a necessary and clear precondition for the achievement of high standards for all students. Advocates of standards in education share with advocates of gender equity a commitment to seeing all students attain the same levels of achievement. This goal does not accept outcomes that vary according to background variables such as gender.

No Single Route to Excellence

But beyond the shared goal of equal achievement, issues become more complex. Ellen Wahl notes that although the meaning of a "good education" probably does not differ for boys or girls, groups of students may very well "need different things to get a good education." What it actually takes for the undifferentiated population of "all students" to achieve the same outcomes will probably vary, in other words, depending on gender and class differences, among others. Ignoring these differences means forfeiting excellence—a point widely missed. Wahl asks, Can an education "be considered excellent if it doesn't reach the majority of students, girls and boys of all backgrounds, abilities, incomes? Can we define equity apart from excellence?"[1] Research on equity in access to resources, classroom interaction, and so on, is therefore not opposed to high standards for all students, but an integral part of the standards agenda itself.

The first part of this chapter describes standards (outcome indicators specific to each discipline) and the ways in which equity concerns have interacted with concern for excellent education over the last five years. The second part of this chapter examines research on the resources, skills, and conditions needed to achieve the related educational goals of equity and excellence. These resources include instructional materials such as textbooks and technology, teaching techniques, and, of course, teachers themselves, trained and prepared in schools of education. This second section examines the insight that although the substance of excellent education and high standards transcends differences between groups of students, what it takes to achieve high standards for all students in the classroom context may vary by group. Attention to standards needs to occur simultaneously with an attention to equity between groups of students—in this case, boys and girls.

Who Are All Students?

The equity concerns that fueled the drive for standards early in the 1990s are being overshadowed by a rhetoric that neglects the needs of specific groups of students. Few curriculum standards acknowledge equity problems. Among states that have adopted standards containing equity language, few have developed implementation strategies to ensure that all students can reach the new standards.

In 1992 educational standards were in place for one discipline: mathematics. In 1998 fourteen different sets of standards exist, including one or more for every major discipline: mathematics; science; English language arts; arts education;

history; social studies; geography; physical education; economics; and foreign language.[2]

Equity, however, is not typically featured as an inherent component of realizing high standards. The National Council of Teachers of Mathematics (NCTM) standards have addressed equity more directly than most other initiatives, speaking clearly to the traditional disadvantages that girls and minorities face in mathematics. In addition, NCTM has a specific "equity standard" in its assessment section, and it encourages more than one type of assessment to capture the skills of all types of learners.[3] While the mathematics standards specifically speak to helping girls achieve to higher levels, other national standards, such as the language arts standards, do not confront equity problems. For example, there is no corresponding recognition in the language arts standards of the gender gap in reading, literacy, and other communications skills.

Outstanding examples of state standards that do feature gender equity include New Jersey's systemic initiative, which has integrated gender standards throughout its mathematics and science reform, and Ohio and Colorado's standards.[4] However, most states do not address equity, much less gender equity, in a comprehensive manner to embody the original intentions of the movement.[5]

Regardless of how national organizations or states fashion their standards on paper, the true test of their effectiveness rests on instruction, implementation, and accountability. Inherent in the new standards-based conception of education is a recognition that our current teaching and learning practices must change to actually achieve higher goals. Among those states that have mentioned equity specifically in their standards, few have developed implementation strategies to make sure that all students can reach the new standards.[6] Daniel Humphrey and Patrick Shields reviewed curriculum frameworks in mathematics and science in twelve states, and criticized the treatment of equity in all the examples for lacking "concrete examples and vignettes designed to deal with ... 'implementation of equity-sensitive teaching in the classroom.'"[7] This is particularly disconcerting because the standards movement has its roots in reform efforts to help disadvantaged children achieve to higher levels.[8]

◆　◆　◆

"Calculus in a Pink Ribbon"

When states establish high standards of learning—even when they explicitly acknowledge equity as a precondition for good education—how do they ensure that all students are being held to, and prepared for, these standards in the classroom? Significantly, some research has revealed an alignment between innovative, engaging instructional practices that encourage attainment of high educational standards and instructional practices that encourage gender-equitable teaching.[9] Collaborative group learning, emphasis on practical applications, interdisciplinary approaches, and the placement of science in a more holistic and social context were all outlined initially by scholars from women's studies and ethnic studies and have been applied by the standards movement to advance "excellent education" for the generic "all students."[10]

However, since few of these strategies, when transplanted to the standards movement, are directly linked to the needs of girls or historically disadvantaged groups, their impact and usefulness for these groups may be lost or misinterpreted or even become harmful.[11] Valerie Lee argues, for example, that some strategies, such as making classrooms more "nurturing," merely "wrap calculus in a pink ribbon," and do not constitute useful reform.[12] Similarly, although research has suggested that girls tend to prefer a more cooperative setting rather than the competitive one familiar to many classrooms, evidence indicates that group work in and of itself, without an awareness of classroom gender dynamics, is simply not effective in involving girls.[13] In mixed-sex groups, boys do not work readily with girls, and girls rarely take on leadership roles.[14] Some information about teaching strategies and the groups for whom they are effective is lost between the adoption of national standards and state and classroom interpretations of those standards.

Thus, national standards purport to serve "all students," yet fail to define who these students are. Again, the question is not one of equality (Do girls receive "the same" attention? Are girls equally represented in textbooks? Do teachers understand how to treat girls "the same" as boys?) but of equity. It is a question of appropriateness and balance. Ironically, the very equity concerns that sparked the standards movement earlier in the 1990s are now being lost under a rhetoric that fails to consider what specific groups of students, such as girls, need to achieve an equitable education. Without a simultaneous attention to standards for all students and the advancement of equity for specific groups of students, such as girls and boys, an "excellent education" will remain an elusive goal.

From Standards to the Classroom: What Happens in Schools?

....

Unequal treatment and more subtle forms of classroom bias still discourage the achievement of girls and minorities, particularly in mathematics, science, and technology. Strategies that advance equity have potential to advance high standards for all students, but only if they are implemented with an understanding of specific groups' different classroom needs.

In 1992 *How Schools Shortchange Girls* reported serious inequities in our nation's classrooms. The authors found that (1) girls received less teacher attention than boys, (2) girls received less complex, challenging interaction with their teachers than boys, (3) girls received less constructive feedback from their teachers than boys, (4) girls' responses received less wait-time than boys' responses, and (5) gender bias in teacher-student interaction varied across subject areas, with math and science classes showing the largest inequities. The report also found a relative lack of research on gender bias in teacher-student interaction within specific racial or ethnic groups, citing a few studies that showed that minority students received less attention than white students.

No single culprit keeps students from pursuing and achieving in mathematics, science, and technology—or any other subject, for that matter. Instead, an unwelcoming message is transmitted in myriad subtle ways—through asides, jokes, classroom interactions, and implied meanings, real in their effects but often difficult to pinpoint.[15] Peggy Orenstein observed in 1994, for instance, that it is socially acceptable for boys to ridicule girls and their ideas, particularly in mathematics and science.[16]

◆　◆　◆

....

Living up to Teacher Expectations of Boys and Girls

Research since 1992 on classroom climate contends that what teachers describe as girls' strengths in the classroom—good behavior, the desire to please the teacher, and general attention to assigned tasks—actually works against them; at the same time, boys' poor behavior works in their favor. Teachers direct their attention to students who make noise and cause trouble; generally, these students are male. In contrast, teachers more typically single out girls as the ideal students—neat, responsible, and quiet.[17] Peter Hall, Sherrill Pryor, and Bernice Sandler write, "Teachers are generally tolerant of the status quo"—the fact that some groups of students are silent and some groups dominate the classroom—and "make little attempt to change the behavior of either group."[18] Pryor found that pre-service teachers (teachers still in training) did not know how to address culturally specific behaviors, such as Asian American girls' tendency "not to initiate class discussion until they are called on."[19]

Most of the post-1992 research on classroom interactions has focused on whether girls and boys receive equal amounts and quality of teacher interaction. Qualitative, small-scale studies of the last five years cumulatively describe progress as well as persistent concerns. Carole Shmurak and Thomas Ratliff studied eighty middle-school classrooms, observing teacher practices, student behaviors, instructional materials, and room decorations.[20] They found the math classes were the most equitable in student participation, and language arts had the most male domination, with other subject areas falling somewhere in between. Mary Yepez observed four teachers of English as a Second Language, concluding that three of the four showed "remarkable equality" in their classroom interactions with the boys and girls.[21]

In contrast, Melody D'Ambrosio and Patricia Hammer studied the treatment of girls and boys in forty-one Catholic elementary schools.[22] Echoing earlier work by Myra and David Sadker, they concluded that male students receive more attention in all categories of teacher-student interaction (praise, acceptance, remediation, and criticism).[23] Mary Bendixen-Noe and Lynne Hall, Sandra Zaher, and Charol Shakeshaft reached similar conclusions.[24] Valerie Lee and Helen Marks observed eighty-six classrooms, finding "gender domination" by boys in many classrooms in coeducational schools, particularly in science classes.[25] Additionally, they found "gender reinforcement," or the perpetuation of gender-differentiated behaviors, and "embedded discrimination" in both the single-sex and coed classrooms. This sexism emanated both from teachers and from students, who tend to self-select into groupings and roles according to gender norms.

Significantly, Lee and Marks found that "66 percent of all the sexist incidents in the coeducational classroom occurred in chemistry classes, although these classes constituted only 20 percent of our observations."[26] "Sexist incidents" include the following account from a coeducational chemistry class: "In this class of nine boys and five girls, the male teacher was describing an experiment (to be done by students) involving measuring liquids. His discussion was directed to the boys. A girl in the front row asked for clarification of the use of the graduated cylinder. Since the teacher ignored her inquiry, she repeated her question. The teacher, clearly exasperated with the student, tossed the water in the graduated cylinder onto the girl and her desk. The entire class laughed, and the teacher did nothing to control them. An after-class conversation with this teacher revealed that he believed that girls are not suited to 'do' science."[27]

Lee and Marks also documented some notable examples of equity, "emanating from both students and teachers." Unfortunately these examples "occurred simultaneously" in many classes with the reinforcement of sexism. Examples of equity included teachers who called attention to the clarity and perceptiveness of a female student's comments, and a male student's retort to a female student's complaint that she was "just too dumb" to do math. Replied the boy, "That's no excuse!"[28]

The Best Intentions

The attention that boys receive is not necessarily intended bias against girls.[29] Research suggests that teachers often fail to give girls direct feedback or criticism because they don't want to hurt their feelings or discourage them.[30] But protective attitudes like this often backfire: If girls don't receive feedback in elementary school, they don't learn to respond to criticism.[31] Miller et al. found that teachers' use of follow-up probes was negatively related to females' self-concept, which implies that girls are not accustomed to being challenged in the classroom. Dianne D. Horgan argues that this lack of early exposure to academic argument and challenge translates into later difficulties in self-assessment, both in school and work settings, as girls and women anticipate "ready acceptance" rather than criticism of their work.[32]

In addition to giving boys more attention and feedback, teachers also continue to give boys more time to answer questions than girls. The classroom moves at a fast pace, and teachers usually give students less than a second to answer any given question. If a girl is more concerned about getting the right answer, she may not respond positively to the pressure of answering a question quickly. At the same time boys fail to learn important lessons in self-control, listening skills, and respect for others. Bernice Sandler et al. conclude that "[female and minority] students may equate their own lack of participation with a lack of intellectual competence, thus undermining their own self-confidence."[33]

Other research suggests that African American girls, whose home culture often encourages assertiveness and outgoing behavior, begin school well-equipped to keep up with the fast pace of classroom interaction. However, as they go through the system, some black girls who speak out, drop out, says Michelle Fine.[34] The result, some find, is that, collectively, black girls grow more passive and quiet than almost any other school group.[35]

Girls, however, are not consistently silent. Recent research reveals that girls often recognize gender inequities and insist on being heard in the classroom, albeit with mixed results.[36] Jill Taylor, Carol Gilligan, and Amy Sullivan write about twenty-six low-income and working-class girls within an urban high school.[37] These girls, representing a range of racial and ethnic backgrounds, both voice and silence their thoughts, feelings, and needs with paradoxical outcomes. In her review of the work, Carla O'Connor writes:

> The child-rearing practices that encourage black girls to express "voice and power" may armor them against the symbolic violence of racism, and foster healthy psychological development. However, that same "voice" also places

them at risk for dropping out when it produces psychological isolation and (is realized in) conflict with school officials.[38]

Realizing Equity and Standards

The use of varied and often innovative teaching methods, including hands-on laboratory experiences, collaborative learning, and practical applications group work, has been linked with higher performance for some students in at least some situations. Such strategies also show promise in drawing on the cultural strengths and needs of varied groups of students.

Methods of Teaching and Learning

As is evident in research dealing with classroom climate and interaction, academic success for girls in the traditional classroom structure seems to require, in effect, that they "act like boys."[39] Writes Michele Foster, "Most of what occurs in traditional classrooms encourage[s] competitive behavior and individual achievement."[40] Attempts to treat girls "the same as" other individuals places them at an educational disadvantage if their school values a competitive ethos and if these girls have internalized the idea that girls shouldn't demonstrate competitive or aggressive behavior. The classroom status quo, while it doesn't embody an intentional bias against girls, nevertheless prizes values that still conflict with many girls' perceptions of appropriate feminine behavior. "To simply encourage the expression of ['everyone's'] experiences, or voices," as Frances Maher says, "is in fact to encourage the more privileged voices."[41] The attainment of uniformly high standards by all students requires a more thoughtful approach.

Since 1992 educational critics have advocated a variety of techniques to change basic assumptions about classroom organization and the learning process, rather than simply to better integrate girls as a "special group" into the conventional classroom organization of learning. The innovations include hands-on laboratory experiences, collaborative learning, an emphasis on practical applications group work, and "authentic instruction."[42] Fred Newmann defines authentic instruction as involving "tasks that are considered meaningful, valuable, significant, and worthy of one's effort ... work that entails extrinsic rewards, meets intrinsic interests, offers students a sense of ownership, is connected to the 'real world' (the world beyond school), and involves some fun. ..."[43] The strategies respond to concerns that many groups of students don't learn well by listening passively to instructors—the traditional teaching style. They also respond to the observation that "there is currently more emphasis on the development of assertive than affiliative skills, more reward for solo behavior than collaborative behavior, more reward for speaking than for listening."[44]

Much of the research on teaching and gender equity has focused on math/science education, rather than the full spectrum of content areas.[45] To girls' benefit, a growing movement to keep girls "in the science pipeline" has stimulated research on what actually happens in the classroom to make girls leave science.[46] Here, research has found that pedagogy makes a difference: For example, the use of hands–on lab activities is linked to higher performance for girls.[47] F. Hughes–McDonnell argues that students, particularly girls, seek to be the developers of knowledge, rather than passive receivers of knowledge.[48] She contends that many classrooms are typified by passivity: The teacher lectures, students conduct labs that have specified answers, and the teacher grades on neatness rather than originality. Indeed, one girl said of her science classroom, "I just feel like a visitor in someone else's class."[49] Similar situations appear to occur within the physical education classroom, where Gloria Napper-Owen, Jepkorir Chepyator-Thomson, and Catherine Ennis have noted that class organization, teaching style, teacher-student interactions, role models, and equipment tended to favor boys.[50]

Drawing on Cultural Strengths

Math and science teaching deserves the research attention it has received in the last five years, because it attempts to remedy a well-documented inequity in educational outcome—girls' attrition from two crucial subject areas of the curriculum. However, to achieve the goal of equitable and excellent education, we need to develop a deeper range of pedagogical techniques, not simply to boost girls' performance in math and science, but to "leverage" the particular cultural strengths and needs of different groups of students. The use of varied instructional techniques advances equitable outcomes in education by recognizing what specific groups of students, including girls, realistically need to reach high standards.

For example, potential exists to transform science and mathematics pedagogy generally by borrowing from Native American traditions. As Sharon Nelson-Barber and Elise Estrin write:

> Many American Indian students have extensive knowledge of mathematics and science knowledge that is rooted in naturalist traditions common to Native communities and arrived at through observation and direct experience. Because many Indian communities follow traditional subsistence lifestyles, parents routinely expose their offspring to survival routines, often immersing the children in decision-making situations in which they must interpret new experiences in light of previous ones. Unfortunately, a majority of teachers recognize neither Indian students' knowledge nor their considerable learning strategies. Thus, not only is potentially important content knowledge ignored but well-developed ways of knowing, learning, and problem solving also go unrecognized.[51]

The use of varied instructional techniques not only recognizes different groups' needs; it can draw attention to students' varied strengths. These strengths are often invisible in traditional classrooms that send the message that differences are not important. Michelle Fine, Lois Weis, and Linda C. Powell write: ["The message to] leave your differences at the door reproduces privilege, oppression and opposition in the guise of neutrality or 'color-blindness.'"[52]

Innovative pedagogical strategies, in other words, not only accommodate girls from nonwhite ethnic backgrounds, but can transform classroom interaction positively and consistently for all students, with the goal of achieving high standards through more engaging, rigorous instructional strategies. Some research has shown tremendous achievement gains for black students in schools and classrooms where learning is seen as involving social interaction, "not as a competitive or individual endeavor."[53] Puerto Rican girls belong to a culture

in which "parents value interdependence and nurture cooperation in children."[54] Within current classroom culture, this can
be, and often is, misunderstood. Puerto Rican girls, for example, can appear too passive in the classroom or too helpful or
deferential toward others. Here, the goal should not be for
Puerto Rican girls to conform to classroom norms that require
them to be more competitive and individualistic, but that
notions of valuable styles and successful methods for learning
should become more diverse, eclectic, and accommodating.

Instructional Materials

*Instructional materials such as computers and textbooks need
further attention to advance the dual agenda of equity and educational standards. Textbooks make female characters more visible than they were just a few years ago but still frequently
place girls and women in stereotypical roles. Classroom reliance
on computer technology has increased dramatically but with
little attention to gender differences in computer use. Technology
runs the risk of exacerbating these differences as it becomes
more integral to the K–12 curriculum.*

Textbooks

How Schools Shortchange Girls reviewed twenty years of
research documenting gender bias in textbooks and other
classroom materials, major sources of curricular guidance for
instructors and students. Prior studies of educational reform,
it noted, failed to examine the equity content of textbooks,
classroom materials, technological software, or other curriculum materials.[55]

Today's textbooks are far less sexist and racist than those of
the 1970s, and somewhat more balanced than were texts in
1992. Textbook producers have made a greater effort to
include women and to reflect female as well as male perspectives on topics covered. Reviewers of new history textbooks
have found a much greater emphasis on women and minorities.[56] Carole Shmurak and Thomas Ratcliff contend that middle school textbook publishers have made a similar effort to
reflect gender and cultural diversity.[57] Christine Beyer exam-

ined fourteen middle and high school curricula published over ten years, finding greater female representation.[58] Similarly, Gail Goss's research on recommended children's literature notes the emergence of female adventurers and rescuers, and of males who perform household chores and handle child care.

The enhanced ability of such texts to stir girls' imagination and accurately reflect their perceptions of the world they inhabit lays a better groundwork for their attainment of higher standards.

However, some critics say book editors confuse quantity with quality. Textbook producers have introduced gender into their works ambivalently, often placing female characters in stereotypical roles that reinforce the very biases textbooks would transcend.[59] Ideally, equitable textbooks do not merely add women into a traditional historical account, but instead explain to students how contributions made by specific groups are central to the overall historical narrative. As one middle school teacher explains, "if you don't [include] the history of women, you're not really teaching history" because women have contributed substantially to social and political change over time.[60] Ladson-Billings found that innovative teachers, "rather than merely bemoan the fact that their textbooks were out of date ... in conjunction with their students, critiqued the knowledge represented in the textbooks. ... The teachers also brought in articles and papers that represented counter knowledge to help the students develop multiple perspectives on a variety of social and historical phenomena."[61]

HOW MANY FEMALE FIGURES IN HISTORY DO YOU KNOW?

Over the past 20 years, Myra and David Sadker have posed the following challenge to high school students around the country, "In five minutes, name twenty famous U.S. women from past or present—no sports figures, no entertainers, and only presidents' wives who are famous in their own right. Do you think you can do it?"

In the years that Sadker and Sadker have asked this question of high school seniors, only a few have met the challenge. "On average, students can list only four or five women from the entire history of the nation." What does this reflect about how women have been included in our curriculum?

Added Challenge: *Does your ability to generate a list change if asked to name famous African Americans? Women with disabilities? Hispanics?*

Source:
Myra and David Sadker, Failing at Fairness: How Our Schools Cheat Girls. (New York: A Touchstone Book, 1995).

Increasingly, school districts are becoming sensitive to the need to have school texts reflect the diversity of their students. In March 1998, in a move that drew nationwide attention, the San Francisco Board of Education unanimously voted to make the high school reading list more multicultural: The board mandated that at least one of seven books chosen by English teachers to be read in class each year be written by authors of color.[62]

Technology

Ten years ago few people would have imagined students logging on to the Internet from school. In 1998 computers have become commonplace in many classrooms, as early as kindergarten in some cases. In 1996, 65 percent of U.S. public schools had access to the Internet—a 15 percent gain over each of the two preceding years.[63] The Texas Board of Education has seriously considered buying no more costly textbooks and instead giving each public school student his or her own laptop computer. Computer technology, the board argued, could give students access to the most current and extensive bodies of knowledge for an upgrade of $1.25, rather than being tethered to quickly obsolete and expensive textbooks.[64]

Computer technology is the cutting-edge—and seductive—instructional resource for 21st-century education, yet its optimal applications for instruction and education have yet to be determined. As 1997 Educational Testing Service research discovered, school districts have invested millions, even billions, of dollars in wiring schools, yet apparently lack a deep understanding of "how technology is being used for and by different types of students."[65] However, educators, administrators, and policymakers have energetically and consistently promoted technology as a tool that might level class and race inequities in educational achievement. The 1997 President's Commission on Technology and K–12 Education concluded that the potential of computer technology to "empower historically disadvantaged groups ... with greater access to knowledge building and communication tools" can "scarcely be overstated." The Texas Board of Education championed its proposal to equip students with laptops on the grounds it would undercut differences between wealthy and poor students. "They're going to have an equal shot," explained the

Texas board chair. "All of a sudden everyone starts at the same starting line. I truly believe it's going to occur within the next six years."[66]

Access to computers may indeed equalize some educational inequities between wealthy and poor students, but boys and girls—rarely a focus of equity discussions concerning education and technology—are not necessarily at the same starting line when it comes to the use of computer tools.

Sandra Hanson cautions that rectifying the gender imbalance in technology experience, course taking, use, and interest does not entail "fixing the student," but rather, examining the "psychological, social, attitudinal, and environmental [factors]" that limit girls' interest in and opportunities to use technology.[67] Students carry many of these social and attitudinal factors into the classroom from their larger social and familial worlds. Boys enter the classroom with more prior experience with computers and other technology than girls, and in turn interact more positively and proactively with technology in the classroom. Boys visit computer exhibits in science museums more often and attentively than do girls.[68] Toy stores place computer toys in the "boys' aisles," as most companies market them primarily to boys.[69]

Within the classroom, girls react differently to computer technology than boys, leading some researchers to write about "masculine" and "feminine" ways of interacting with computers.[70] Boys describe computers as "enjoyable," "special," "friendly," and "important;" girls, as a population, do not use such inviting terms. In a 1997-98 study of technology use in a large suburban school system, girls of all ethnicities consistently rated themselves significantly lower than boys on computer ability and were less likely than boys to think computers help them do better on schoolwork.[71] The findings are consistent with those based on earlier data: In a meta-analysis of eighty-one studies from 1973 to 1992, Whitley found that boys exhibited greater sex-role stereotyping of computer use, higher computer self-efficacy, and more positive affect about computers than did girls, with the largest differences generally found at the high school level.[72]

Girls interact more routinely with computers in schools than elsewhere, but some technology-based course material may exacerbate rather than diminish gender imbalance. Bias has been documented in technological materials intended for classroom use.[73] A small but purportedly representative study of elementary mathematics software in 1995 found that, of the 40 percent that had gender-identifiable characters, only 12 percent of the characters were female. Furthermore, the the study by Carol Hodes found that the material portrayed these female characters passively in the stereotypical roles of mother and princess. In stark contrast, male characters appeared as "heavy equipment operators, factory workers, shopkeepers, mountain climbers, hang gliders, garage mechanics, and one program used a male genie to give directions."[74] Staci Durham and Sheila Brownlow examined children's cartoons and discovered that, as in textbooks, the material both reinforced and challenged sex-appropriate behaviors regarding the use of technology. Despite the positive portrayal of female characters in some episodes, their appearance was rare and they were usually not the main focus of action.[75]

Not surprisingly, given the emphasis on technology as a masculine domain, many girls in high school forgo the opportunity to take computing classes that could lead to technology careers. (See Chapter 1). The gender gap widens from grade eight to grade eleven.[76] In 1996 only 17 percent of high school students taking the advanced placement computer science exam were female—a statistic essentially unchanged from the previous year.[77] Because few women train as computer software designers or programmers, the cycle of technological innovations created by men—and often targeted to men and boys—repeats itself.

As a whole, research shows that girls have developed an appreciably different relationship to technology than boys, and that as a result, technology may exacerbate rather than diminish inequities by gender as it becomes more integral to the K–12 curriculum. The difference is not only in the dearth of realistic female images in software and games, but in girls' overall attitude and orientation toward technology.

Cornelia Brunner envisions the equity agenda in technology and instruction as a process of educating girls, in particular, to imagine themselves as "power users," capable of generalizing "about human-computer interactions, and thus able to learn new programs on their own." Girls, she says, need to be invited to "think of themselves as potential designers of hardware and software rather than mere 'end users.'"[78] Much more research and action are needed to ensure that girls and women develop such a confident relationship to technology. As Brunner notes, the goal for equity in technology is not so much ensuring equal access to programming skills, but to integrate digital tools "into the curriculum so that girls will be able to use them to pursue their own, genuine interests."[79]

Many predict a more thorough integration of curriculum and technology is inevitable in the next decade. A powerful tool that holds potential for leveling class differences in educational outcomes must not be permitted to become a barrier for gender equity.

Teachers and Teacher Education

....

Equitable teaching is basic to education that aims to offer uniformly high standards. But teachers receive little or no training in equity from schools of education. In a national survey in 1993 and 1994, the largest amount of time teacher educators spent on gender equity was two hours per semester. One-third of the teacher educators surveyed spent one hour or less. The pattern continues despite evidence of the success of teacher equity training.

Research has documented that the entry into teaching in the United States can be overwhelming: Up to 30 percent of teachers leave within the first three years.[80] Much of this attrition has been attributed to the stress of learning basic classroom management, developing a pedagogical style, and compiling the core of a teacher's classroom strategies. Teachers enter the field prepared, for the most part, to accomplish these tasks. However, they do not enter the field prepared to teach in an equitable manner. Therefore, they are not prepared to make changes in school curriculum, interaction patterns, pedagogical strategies, or uses of resources such as technology that would advance equitable learning.

◆ ◆ ◆

....

No Training in Equity

Patricia Campbell and Jo Sanders conducted a national survey of teacher educators in methods in 1993 and 1994 and found that while 72 percent of professors reported doing some gender equity in their methods courses, and another 15 percent said they would like to do so, the largest amount of time spent on gender equity was two hours per semester. Two-thirds (68 percent) spent two hours or less per semester, and a third spent one hour or less. In that hour, professors primarily lectured or talked to their students about gender equity, although nearly half (49 percent) used classroom observations. Coverage centered on stereotypes, followed by teacher/student interaction patterns favoring boys, the underrepresentation of girls in mathematics, science, and technology courses and activities, and the underrepresentation of women in mathematics, science, and technological careers. Perhaps most tellingly, the classes rarely reported practical, gender equity solutions to problems. Of those professors who spent time on gender equity, more than half (55 percent) reported being satisfied with the one or two hours they were including.[81]

Between 1994 and 1996, the Marymount Institute for the Education of Women and Girls obtained virtually identical data that support the need for preservice gender equity training. In a survey of fifty colleges across the nation, the Marymount Institute found that not one offered a course in gender equity as part of its teacher training program; more than 90 percent of the approximately seventy-five faculty members questioned stated that gender equity was merely mentioned in their curricula, and that gender equity was the subject of a "one-hour lecture" during the semester in some programs.[82] In 1993 Jordan Titus also found a general invisibility of gender issues in education "foundations" texts. Where gender differences were portrayed, she found, the texts suggested that "such differences were given, fixed, and determinate." None portrayed a strategy for solving a gender equity problem.[83]

The absence of any discussion of hands-on, practical solutions to equity problems in the classroom is particularly frustrating because research has shown that teachers are both eager and able to change their teaching styles to advance classroom equity when given the chance and the training. In 1997 Sherrill Pryor found that after several viewings of videotapes of classrooms, teachers identified habits—such as giving more feedback and criticism to boys—that unintentionally biased their classrooms. She reported that before any training, "fewer than 60 percent of the preservice teachers were aware of subtler forms of bias, such as the disparity in the number of reprimands of males and females, and the disparity of classroom task assignments between males and females."[84]

Indifference to teacher training for equity may reflect vague teacher certification standards at the national level, as documented by Jacqueline Jones and Edward Chittenden.[85] The new National Council for Accreditation of Teacher Education (NCATE) standards for teacher education, released in fall 1997, include equity as one of five essential attributes.[86] However, they provide little detail on equity indicators or helpful teaching techniques.[87]

Some educators assume that equitable teaching is just good teaching and is thereby implicit in good teacher training. Here, again, the difference must be emphasized between excellent education—presumably the same thing for boys and girls—and what it takes to achieve that education for specific groups. Although equitable teaching is one aspect of good teaching, the practice must be learned. Equity is not automatic—even to female teachers. Sanders argues that "teacher education is the point at which future educators are accessible ... are there to learn, have time to learn, and don't have years of bad teaching habits to undo."[88] It is more difficult to reach practicing teachers. Professional development reached slightly more than 50 percent of teachers in the 1993-94 school year; teacher education reaches 100 percent, every year.[89]

In 1998 the movement to incorporate equity into teacher education is growing. Sanders, Campbell, and Karin Steinbrueck reported successful results from the Teacher Education Equity Project (TEEP).[90] A program designed to "promote gender equity in mathematics, science, and technology education at the source," TEEP worked with sixty-one professors in colleges of education across the United States. As a result of this project, 85 percent of the participants adopted more equitable practices, and professors dramatically increased the specific gender equity activities they reported doing with their classes. Pre- and post- measures of syllabi also showed significant gains on course descriptions, gender equity readings, and gender equity assignments. The greatest gains were in the most substantive measure: assignments. By the follow-up, the percentage of syllabi including gender equity assignments had tripled, to 36 percent.[91]

Unfortunately, while this and other teacher training efforts show promise, such efforts are rare and sometimes belittled. When Titus introduced gender equity topics throughout the curriculum in a foundations course, she encountered resistance from students and professors.[92] Colleges of education, as portals into the classroom, equip teachers with tools to develop their classroom style and content, and to evaluate their own teaching—except in this critical area. Here, colleges often lack professorial and student support. According to Susan Bailey, one of the most important steps educators can take to reduce gender inequity in schools is to support faculty development programs.[93] Campbell and Sanders write convincingly that "it is unnecessary, year after year, to graduate new classroom teachers who, because they do not know any better, unintentionally diminish the educational, career, and economic prospects of females and thus of the nation."[94]

Summary

The proliferation of curriculum standards, now covering every major discipline, marks a new development in the quest for educational excellence. But as it gains momentum, the standards movement appears in growing danger of losing sight of the varying needs of different student groups.

Equity, the erasure of differences in outcome by social factors such as race, class, or gender, is a precondition for the achievement of high standards for all students. Ironically, the very equity concerns that sparked the standards movement earlier in the 1990s are now being lost under a rhetoric that fails to consider what specific groups of students, such as girls, need to achieve a uniformly excellent education.

Few standards, as written, acknowledge equity issues. Mathematics standards are better than most, clearly addressing traditional disadvantages faced by girls and minorities. In contrast, language arts standards say nothing of the gender gap in reading, literacy, and other communications skills.

Among states that have adopted standards containing equity language, few have developed implementation strategies to ensure that all students can reach the new standards.

Adapting goals of equitable and excellent education to classroom realities involves a host of additional challenges. Since 1992 researchers and educators have examined a variety of instructional strategies, spurred by concern that some groups of students—including girls in math and the sciences—have been underserved by conventional, lecture-driven classroom styles. Alternate, often innovative, teaching approaches challenge some of the underlying principles about how classrooms should be organized. Strategies that advance equity also have deep potential to advance high standards for all students, but only if they are implemented with an understanding of specific groups' different classroom needs.

Instructional resources, such as computers and textbooks, also need attention. While textbooks have become more gender-conscious in recent years, many still place female characters in stereotypical roles that reinforce biases. At the same time, computer technology is a seductive classroom resource, but one that involves a gender imbalance favoring boys in experience, use, course taking, and interest. Consequently, technology may exacerbate rather than diminish inequities by gender as it becomes more integral to the curriculum.

Excellent education—education that prepares all students to meet high standards—requires equitable teaching. But teachers, because they receive little or no training in equity from schools of education, enter the field unprepared to teach in an equitable manner. In a national survey of teacher educators in 1993 and 1994, researchers found that the largest amount of time spent on gender equity was two hours per semester. If we are going to give more than lip service to the twin goals of classroom equity and academic excellence, teacher education will have to encompass training in equity.

◆ ◆ ◆

Recommendations

- Producers and purchasers of educational materials should establish processes and criteria by which to screen curricula and instructional materials for bias in images, text, or logic.
- States that adopt standards must develop implementation strategies to ensure that all students can reach the new standards.
- Equity must be viewed as integral to teacher education and the achievement of educational excellence and must be integrated into preservice training.
- Preservice practicums and/or student teaching experiences should provide teachers with experience in working with a wide variety of students.
- Teachers need guidance on how to integrate technology into the entire school curriculum to advance the dual goals of excellent and equitable education.
- Educators need to examine and disseminate methods behind exemplary efforts, like the Teacher Education Equity Project, to promote the teaching of gender equity to faculty in colleges.
- The National Council for Accreditation of Teacher Education standards need to make explicit what is meant by "equity" and provide indicators to determine whether education departments are meeting these equity standards.
- As this report has confirmed, classroom interaction and experience remains a critical, but elusive piece of the equity agenda. Researchers should undertake more systematic classroom interaction studies, which utilize standard indicators of equity to facilitate comparisons and synthesis across the field of smaller studies. Indicators or questions to consider in qualitative classroom interaction research include: teacher expectations for all students, teaching strategies and methods that address the learning styles of all students, a teacher's degree and level of interaction with boys and girls, and classroom behavior between peers.

CHAPTER FOUR

Educational Risks and Resiliency

◆

Why do some girls succeed while others in the same school environments do not? Achievements and failures in school almost invariably have some origins in social, communal, and familial worlds outside of the school. Research shows that these external factors profoundly influence educational outcomes. However, schools can and do intervene to modify individual risk factors, particularly as these impinge on the learning process and educational outcomes. Two areas in which school practices profoundly shape girls' experiences are grade repetitions and dropping out—where school policies affect girls' willingness to stay in school. This chapter will examine these two areas.

Risk factors and dangers do not entirely control girls' outcomes. Risks are just that: chances, some stronger than others, that a girl will encounter educational difficulties. But not all at-risk students experience academic difficulties, nor do all students who experience academic difficulties subsequently drop out. While 27 percent of grade repeaters eventually dropped out, the majority, 73 percent, did not. Many resilient and resistant girls achieve in the face of opposition. This chapter will explore recent research on the sources of strength that allow groups of students to overcome risks and prevail.

◆ ◆ ◆

Repeating Grades and Dropping Out

Boys repeat grades and drop out of school at a higher rate than girls. However, the link between grade repetition and dropping out is stronger for girls than boys. In other words, girls who are held back a grade are more likely to drop out at some point in their academic careers than boys who are held back. Not only does there appear to be something particularly detrimental to girls about being held back; there is something more detrimental to girls about dropping out: Girls who drop out are less likely than their male counterparts to return and complete school.

Examined by race and class, grade retention and dropout rates show other disturbing patterns. Black and low-income students are retained at a higher rate than others. The dropout rate among Hispanic girls is startlingly high: In 1995, 30 percent of Hispanic females age 16 to 24 had dropped out of school and not yet passed a high school equivalency test.

In 1990 Michelle Fine wrote that dropouts should be called "push-outs" instead because schools give these students little encouragement to stay enrolled. Specific reasons vary, case by case, but the underlying logic is the same: In the minds of school administrators, some students don't fit the system. Girls and boys continue to show different risks of academic failure, expressed through repeating grades and dropping out.[1]

In their foreword to a curriculum guide published in 1996 by the California Latino-Chicano High School Dropout Prevention Project, Ray del Portillo and Margot M. Segura describe common patterns of school dropouts:

> The profile of the dropout, as well as many school-related factors in the dropout (or "pushout") rate, has remained constant for the last 50 years: frequent absences from class; lack of basic academic skills; frequent residential changes; the inability to relate to authority figures; and lack of language fluency. Simply put, a student who speaks English and/or Spanish poorly, who moves often and never puts down roots in a school or community, and who has problems learning in a traditional classroom setting, has many obstacles to overcome in order to succeed in school.[2]

All of these variables are highly correlated with socioeconomic status (SES). And of all the factors in the mix, SES is by far the most powerful predictor of school success or failure. But this connection does not account for differences in the dropout patterns of girls and boys. Since girls and boys are equally represented among low-SES groups, we have to look further for an explanation of why the link between grade repetition and dropping out is stronger for girls than boys.

How Schools Shortchange Girls, citing the 1988 National Educational Longitudinal Study, reported that girls of low socioeconomic status were more likely to do well than low-SES boys, while girls of high socioeconomic status were only as likely and often less likely to do as well as boys. The NELS data also showed that among low-SES students, boys are more likely than girls to have repeated at least one grade. This holds almost equally true for black, white, and Hispanic boys. Among low-SES students, regardless of race or ethnicity, boys are more likely than girls to have repeated at least one grade. There is more similarity between male and female retention rates among low SES black students than between low SES males and females of other racial groups.[3]

In 1995, 17 percent of males and 10 percent of females age 16 to 24 had been retained, with most retentions occurring in kindergarten through third grade. Similarly, schools retained black and low-income students at a higher rate than students from other racial-ethnic and socioeconomic backgrounds. Grade repetitions thus appear to be more of a risk for boys than for girls, a problem of uneven educational outcomes by gender that merits further investigation. Students run the highest risk of a grade repetition in first grade. Boys are more likely than girls to repeat first grade as well as other grades in their academic careers.[4] (See Table 16.)

Dropout rates are also generally higher for males than females. White females continue to have the lowest dropout rate of any racial or gender group. However, between 1980 and 1995 the proportion of Hispanic females dropping out of school has been consistently high. In 1995, 30 percent of Hispanic females age 16 to 24 had dropped out of school and not yet passed a high school equivalency test. In contrast, dropout rates have remained stable for white males and females and black males; dropout rates have declined for

Table 16
Grade Retention Rates by Gender, Race-Ethnicity, and Income (Age 16–24)

| | 1992 | | | | 1995 | | | |
Characteristic	Percent Retained	Grade of last retention K-3	4-8	9-12	Percent Retained	Grade of last retention K-3	4-8	9-12
Total	11.1	4.1	2.7	2.2	13.3	6.1	3.3	2.4
Gender								
Male	14.2	5.1	3.3	2.7	16.9	7.3	4.2	3.2
Female	8.1	3.0	2.1	1.7	9.6	4.9	2.4	1.6
Race-ethnicity								
White, non-Hispanic	10.2	4.1	2.3	1.7	12.1	6.2	2.9	2.0
Black, non-Hispanic	17.4	5.2	5.0	3.8	18.7	7.0	5.0	3.7
Hispanic	10.4	3.1	2.5	2.8	14.7	5.7	3.8	3.0
Income*								
Low	15.8	4.6	4.7	3.6	18.2	7.2	5.0	4.0
Middle	11.0	4.2	2.7	2.0	13.1	6.2	3.2	2.3
High	7.7	3.2	1.2	1.4	9.1	5.0	1.8	1.2

Source:
U.S. Department of Education Dropout Rates in the United States: 1995

* Low income=bottom 20 percent of all family incomes for 1991 and 1994.
Middle income is between bottom 20 percent and top 20 percent of family incomes.
High income=top 20 percent of family incomes.

Hispanic males and black females. Language barriers to learning among non-English-speaking Hispanic immigrant students may be contributing to their high dropout rate.[5]

Students who repeat a grade are at significant risk of dropping out later in their academic careers. In 1995 individuals
who had repeated a grade constituted 13 percent of the population but 27 percent of those who had dropped out. A significant gender difference, however, appears in the relationship
between repeating a grade and dropping out. While more boys
repeat a grade and drop out of school, the link between grade
repetitions and subsequent dropping out is stronger among
girls than boys. According to the U.S. Department of
Education, approximately 10 percent of males and females
who never repeated a grade eventually dropped out. However,
22 percent of males and 28 percent of females ever retained
eventually dropped out.[6] The finding implies that there is
something especially detrimental to girls about being held
back, or, alternately, that there is something less detrimental
to boys about being held back. In fact, the finding might reflect

schools' pattern of holding back academically competent male athletes to enhance their playing time. Male students retained for such reasons would be expected to be at less risk for dropping out.[7]

Dropping out is associated further with different disadvantages for girls and boys, since girls are less likely to return and complete school. In 1995 females comprised 45 percent of 15- to 24-year-olds who dropped out that year; they made up 50 percent of 16- to 24-year-olds who stayed out.[8]

Family and Individual Risk Factors

The cumulative effect of poverty, abuse, and other family or community problems that put students at risk takes a higher toll on girls' health than boys'. According to one study, one in five girls has been sexually or physically abused, one in four shows signs of depression, and one in four does not get needed health care. In boys, substance abuse is tied to a higher rate of dropping out; in girls, it is tied to a higher rate of criminality. Sexual harassment makes learning difficult for both girls and boys. Only 8 percent of respondents to a 1993 study reported that their schools possessed and enforced a policy on sexual harassment.

Family risk factors, including poverty, low socioeconomic status, poor parental education, loose family structure, geographic mobility, and a history of abuse or neglect, influence not only the home environment but the educational resources available to the students and their parents' interaction with schools.[9] On top of individual risk factors, some girls face a daunting set of obstacles. Aside from the overarching risk of low SES, or poverty, the four most serious risks to girls' health and education are pregnancy, drug and alcohol use, depression, and delinquency.

Research by the Commonwealth Fund in 1997 found that one in five girls says she has been sexually or physically abused (usually, by family members), one out of four shows signs of depression, and one in four does not get health care when she needs it. The report describes a compounding effect for all these

Skirting Sexuality, Health, and Violence

1992 Goal: *A critical goal of education reform must be to enable students to deal effectively with the realities of their lives, particularly in areas such as sexuality and health.* (How Schools Shortchange Girls, page 88)

Analysis: The 1992 report *How Schools Shortchange Girls* found a lack of enforcement of sexual harassment policies, evaded topics such as violence, power relations, and sexuality, as well as bias in teen "parent" programs. It called for strong policies on sexual harassment to be developed and enforced, multi-institutional responses to sexuality and health issues and comprehensive school-based health and sex-education programs from K-12. Regarding pregnancy, it recommended policies including child care to encourage young mothers to complete school without sacrificing the quality of their education. In 1993 *Hostile Hallways* found that sexual harassment was prevalent in school.

1998 Reality: Some interventions have been developed to deal with student sexuality and health issues, particularly drugs, alcohol, and violence. However, the success of these interventions is not clear, and many areas still are not addressed, routinely if at all, within the school curriculum.

risk characteristics. For example, it notes, "nearly half of the abused girls who had symptoms of depression had gone without health care." The cumulative effect of these risk factors imperils high school girls' self-esteem far more than boys', the report finds: "Adolescents' responses to questions related to mental and physical health indicate that the adolescent years are a far more negative time for girls' health than for boys'." *The Commonwealth Fund Survey of the Health of Adolescent Girls* underscores that the risks girls face often differ, in kind or magnitude, from those faced by boys.[10]

Pregnancy, delinquency, and depression have been consistently linked with poor school performance.[11] As one health director comments, "early parenting and sexual activity will interfere with children's success in school, so that makes it a school issue."[12] "The younger the pregnant adolescent is, the more likely it is that she will never complete the twelfth grade," say Claire Brindiz and Susan Philliber.[13] Pregnancy and delinquency rates are higher among black and Hispanic females than white females. Similarly, pregnancy and delinquency rates are higher among females from families with lower incomes and lower levels of parental education. Researchers disagree on the variance of depression across racial/ethnic and socioeconomic categories.[14] Notably, depression affects more boys than girls prior to adolescence.[15]

The link between substance use and dropping out appears to be stronger for boys, and the link between substance use and criminality appears stronger for girls.[16] While one recent longitudinal study found a significant link for both girls and boys between substance use and dropping out, a large national sample found a significant link only for boys.[17] The relationship between substance use and poor school performance is less clear.

Sexual Harassment

Another risk, not typically grouped with these, is sexual harassment in the schools. *Hostile Hallways*, a 1993 AAUW Educational Foundation survey, found that four out of five public school students from eighth to eleventh grade reported experiencing sexual harassment, defined as "unwanted and unwelcome sexual behavior that interferes with your life." The gender gap among the 81 percent of students who reported having been harassed was surprisingly narrow (85 percent of girls to 76 percent of boys). Girls and boys reported frequent experience as both the targets and perpetrators of harassment: two-thirds of all boys and more than half of all girls surveyed admit that they have sexually harassed someone in school.[18]

Harassment is a striking example of how a risk factor can be related to gender—as in the sexual taunting of boys as "fags" or "sissies" and girls as "dykes"—without its being relevant only to girls, or to boys. In fact, boys and girls are both implicated in the social rituals of peer harassment of a sexual nature, although the consequences for girls may be more severe.[19] Sexual harassment, in other words, corrodes the atmosphere for learning for all students. Girls and boys both suffer in such an environment.

WHEN ARE SCHOOLS LIABLE FOR STUDENT SEXUAL HARASSMENT?

School districts are not liable for a teacher's sexual harassment of a student unless a district official knows of the abuse and does nothing to stop it, ruled the U.S. Supreme Court in June 1998. The 5-to-4 decision in the case of a Texas high school student seduced by her social studies teacher was a setback for those trying to hold schools accountable for curbing student harassment, reported on the rise.

Dissenting justices in Gebser v. Lago Vista Independent School District said the ruling guts the high court's 1992 decision in Franklin v. Gwinnett County. The 1992 ruling held that sexual harassment of a student by a teacher creates a hostile environ-

continued . . .

. . . continued from previous page

ment, in violation of Title IX. It was the first decision that held schools responsible and liable for sexual harassment.

A 1996 ruling by the Eleventh Circuit Court of Appeals applied that interpretation to student to student harassment. The court ruled that "school district liability could be found if the district or its employees knew, or should have known, of the harassment and failed to take prompt and appropriate action to stop it."

The legal language of this case and the clinical way that it has been analyzed mask the very real experiences of girls who are harassed in schools. Nan Stein writes about Katy Lyle, a 15-year-old high school student, who was the target of both verbal and written harassment—graffiti—for sixteen months.

"Statements like 'Katy does it with farm animals,' 'Katy is a slut,' 'Katy gives good head,' and 'Katy sucked my dick after she sucked my dog's dick' remained up on the walls for a period of sixteen months, despite repeated requests from Katy and her parents to the principal to have them removed. His responses included, 'No one reads it anyhow,' and 'It'll make you a strong person.' ... Boys would yell out across the hallways, 'Hey, Katy, I took a leak in your stall today,' and girls would wonder aloud what Katy had done to 'deserve' this.

"Katy was tormented daily on the school bus and as she entered the school. Finally, her older brother, home from college during a vacation, removed the graffiti in a matter of minutes. Although the physical evidence was removed, the taunting continued."

Source:

Nan Stein, "Sexual Harassment in School: The Public Performance of Gendered Violence," *Harvard Educational Review* 65 (1995)2: 145-162.

School adults do little to stop it, according to *The Girls Report*, published in June 1998 by the National Council for Research on Women. Teachers and school officials often stand by as students are harassed in their presence in classrooms and hallways. When school adults intervene, they tend to do so privately, on a case-by-case basis, rather than make incidents a matter of institutional policy.[20]

Table 17 illustrates that girls are at risk in a number of ways in schools, only a few of which have been studied in detail, and only a few of which are understood as occurring at different rates and with different effects for boys and girls.[21] (See Table 17.)

Table 17
Snapshot of Relative Risks by Gender

Students Who...

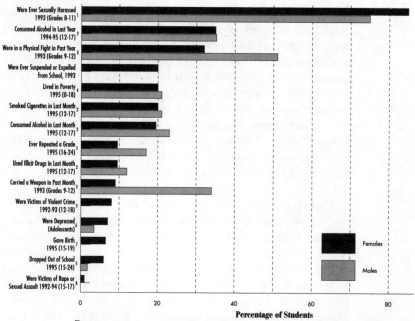

Percentage of Students

Sources:

[1]AAUW (1993) Hostile Hallways; [2]Substance Abuse and Mental Health Services Administration (1997) Substance Abuse Among Women; [3]Girls Incorporated (1996) Prevention and Parity: Girls in Juvenile Justice. Indianapolis, IN: Author; [4]Bryson (1997); [5]U.S. Department of Education (1997) Dropout Rates in the United States: 1995; [6]National Mental Health Organization (1997) Factsheet: Children's and Adolescents' Mental Health; [7]Kirby (1997) No Easy Answers; [8]Perkins (1997) Age Patterns of Victims of Serious Violent Crime, Bureau of Justice Statistics Special Report, July.

Note: Information on percentage of males suspended or expelled was not reported.

There are several caveats to bear in mind when interpreting this exhibit: (1) different sources and, thus, different samples were used; (2) studies collected information from different age ranges of students; (3) studies occurred in different years; (4) studies used different measures of risk (ever vs. past year vs. past month); and (5) studies employed different data collection procedures (self-report vs.transcripts).

Beating the Odds: Resiliency Research and School Programs to Counter Risk

Not all students succumb to the stresses they face. School programs have the potential to help students develop strengths to overcome risks and succeed. AIDS education programs have been credited with slowing the AIDS epidemic. It is unclear whether programs to modify teen sexual behavior have played a role in slowing the teen pregnancy rate. In 1996, 55 percent of all pregnant women were teenagers, compared with 1991, when 62 percent were teens. The number of births to teens also declined. Hispanic teens, however, registered no such birth rate decline. Abstinence-only programs are not consistently effective in urging students to delay sexual intercourse.

A relatively new body of literature has begun to investigate resistance and resiliency—"why certain children who are exposed to significant stresses do not develop severe psychological, learning, or behavioral patterns."[22] Resiliency researchers argue that there is more to be learned and gained from a focus on a population's cultural and social successes than a focus on their failures.[23] As Serge Madhere and Douglas Mac Iver urge, "we must always begin with the assets that students, families, and communities bring to the educational process, and work to equalize and heighten educational outcomes through building on those strengths."[24]

Studies have examined resiliency among diverse groups of girls: gifted urban girls; urban disadvantaged girls; disadvantaged Hispanic girls; and teenage mothers.[25] In a study of Latino and Latina college students, Adele Arellano and Amado Padilla found that goal orientation, high self-esteem, and ability to interpret even very negative experiences into goal-directed actions for success are typical of students who have developed personal qualities and coping skills that act as protective resources.[26] They found no differences between male and female students in resiliency. These findings may also be applicable to younger students. Shwu-yong Huang and Hersholt Waxman found that resilient Mexican Americans reported higher levels of educational support from their teachers and friends; in addition, fewer resilient students had been held back, had gaps in attendance, or were unsure that they would graduate from high school.[27]

Janie Ward's research on African American youth exemplifies the resiliency approach to minimizing risk factors such as violence in the community. Ward explains that "what has been lost to African American youth enmeshed in the violence of U.S. society" is an awareness that "aggression is a violation of the care and connectedness implicit in the notion of black racial identity and community." She contends that a solution to youth violence may lie in reconnecting African American teens to communal values inherent in their cultural heritage and history.[28]

Michael Rutter describes four processes that protect against risk and promote resilience: reduction of risk impact by altering either the risk or exposure to risk; reduction of negative chain reactions that follow risk exposure; establishment and maintenance of self-esteem and self-efficacy; and opening up of opportunities.[29]

Schools can play a role in developing the strengths associated with resiliency. Taken as a whole, these studies suggest specific school-related protective factors that encourage educational achievement among girls who have various risk factors: family involvement and/or support of school success; a school support system (teachers, counselors, coaches) that provides encouragement and role models; a peer group of other successful students; participation in extracurricular activities; participation in special programs (summer enrichment, community, church-based); and participation in academic or honors programs (vs. vocational or other low tracks). Schools attempt to ameliorate individual and social risk factors most directly through curricular and program interventions, particularly programs to modify sexual behavior. Curricular responses to address pregnancy, drug and alcohol use, and sexual harassment vary in duration (one day versus several years), populations targeted (all students versus at-risk students), and goals (increasing knowledge versus changing behavior).[30]

The Teen Pregnancy Problem

The teenage pregnancy rate has declined "slowly but steadily" for the five years between 1991 (when 62 percent of all preg-

nant women were teenagers) and 1996 (when 55 percent were teens) according to the National Center for Health Statistics.

The actual number of births to teens decreased as well, and cannot be discounted as a function of a population decline. As the nonprofit research organization Child Trends documents, "Teens of all ages experienced the decline. Since the number of teenagers is increasing, the slight decline in the number of teen births is due to the falling teen birth rate."[31] The teen birth rate dropped by 17 percent among non-Hispanic blacks, and by more than 9 percent among non-Hispanic whites. There was no similar decline in birth rates for Hispanic teens. "Many [pregnancy prevention programs] are not geared to address the needs" or cultural strengths of Hispanics, although that group is overrepresented in the teen pregnancy statistics.[32]

It is unclear whether or not education, or school interventions, have contributed to the overall decline in teenage pregnancy. Thorough, methodologically sound evaluations of sex education programs are rare. Nonetheless, research has highlighted several shortcomings of current sex education curriculum: length or timing (too little, too late); lack of teacher training and materials; and the relative absence of a focus on male responsibility.[33]

Some health education curricula, mostly those geared toward adolescents, seek to increase knowledge about prevention of sexually transmitted diseases and pregnancy, while others promote abstinence. One of the few conclusions that can be drawn from research is that abstinence-only programs are not consistently effective in urging students to delay sexual intercourse.[34] Some programs that encourage abstinence but also provide information on birth control and the prevention of sexually transmitted diseases have been shown to reduce sexual behavior and increase condom and contraceptive use, but those programs are highly controversial.[35] Douglas Kirby argues that high school sex education programs as currently practiced are unlikely to "make a dent" in the teenage pregnancy rate.[36]

Among all interventions, AIDS education programs have been particularly successful.[37] Future research and program assessment should identify the characteristics of these especially effective AIDS education programs so that they might be replicated in other sex education contexts.

Crucially, and troublingly, sex education school initiatives tend to place primary responsibility for adolescent pregnancy on girls, while boys'—or in many cases, older men's—sexual behavior goes relatively unmodified and unchecked. As one review describes, "girls shoulder the responsibility for not getting pregnant, the blame for getting pregnant, the guilt for having an abortion, and the pressure to give up the child for adoption." It is ironic that "abstention-focused" programs, steeped in an ethic of individual responsibility, have spent little time on boys' and men's personal responsibilities.[38]

Two programs stand out, in contrast, for their more holistic approach to risks, such as pregnancy and sexual harassment, typically thought only to affect and endanger girls as a population. The Bully-Proof curriculum against sexual harassment and the Empower Program, designed to prevent violence, both recognize that boys as well as girls have to change their behaviors to ameliorate risk factors such as teen pregnancy and sexual harassment. Bully-Proof, a curriculum developed by Nan Stein, teaches elementary students the boundaries between teasing and bullying as a way to prevent future harassment.[39] The curriculum is meant for both boys and girls, and involves both groups in solving the problems of bullying and harassment. The Empower Program helps schools and local and national organizations develop violence-prevention programs for young people. Girls' programs focus on the continuum of self-esteem and boundary-setting to sexual harassment, sexual assault, and domestic violence. Boys' programs examine the conventions of masculinity and their influences on male behavior.[40]

When schools have addressed risks through formal curricula, they have not consistently done so in a balanced manner across the sexes, nor have they typically built upon the findings of resiliency research: They have not tried to begin with the strengths of at-risk or historically disadvantaged groups. Although more schools are adopting disciplinary policies for drug and alcohol abuse, administrative responses to sexual harassment and teen pregnancy have been mixed. While more schools have sexual harassment policies, they are generally not well publicized nor consistently enforced. Only 8 percent of respondents to a 1993 study by the NOW Legal Defense and Education Fund and the Wellesley College Center for Women reported that their schools possessed and enforced a policy on sexual harassment.[41] Where sexual harassment policies exist, schools are more likely to take action against harassers.[42] Similarly, administrative barriers and policies (such as inflexible scheduling, crediting, and attendance policies) still exist that deny pregnant and parenting teens the same education as their peers.[43]

Summary

This chapter adds to the analysis of the ways in which schools intervene in, and constrain, educational equity. School actions put boys at greater risk of being retained a grade, while more girls who are retained eventually drop out. Schools limit gender equity in outcomes, too, when they fail to confront or discuss external risk factors for students, such as violence, sexuality, and health concerns.

Boys run a higher risk than girls for both repeating grades and dropping out. In 1995, 17 percent of males and 10 percent of females age 16 to 24 had been retained, most often in kindergarten through third grade. Black and low-income students are retained at a higher rate than others. Boys drop out at higher rates than girls, too. However, the link between grade repetition and dropping out is stronger among girls than boys.

The cumulative effect of poverty, abuse, and other family or community problems that put students at risk takes a higher toll on girls' health than boys'. According to one study, one in five girls has been sexually or physically abused, one in four shows signs of depression, and one in four does not get needed health care. In boys, substance abuse is tied to a higher rate of dropping out; in girls, it is tied to a higher rate of criminality. Sexual harassment makes learning difficult for both girls and boys. Only 8 percent of respondents to a 1993 study reported that their schools possessed and enforced a policy on sexual harassment.

Not all students succumb to the stresses they face. In some cases, schools have developed programs to intervene against risks, although it is not yet clear how widespread such programs are. It is also not clear to what extent these programs build on girls'—or boys'—strengths.

AIDS education programs have been credited with slowing the AIDS epidemic. It is unclear whether programs to modify teen sexual behavior have played a role in slowing the teen pregnancy rate. In 1996, 55 percent of all pregnant women were teenagers, compared with 1991, when 62 percent were teens. The number of births to teens also declined. Hispanic teens, however, registered no such birth rate decline. Abstinence-only programs are not consistently effective in urging students to delay sexual intercourse.

Sex education school initiatives tend to place primary responsibility for adolescent pregnancy on girls, and give scant attention to male behavior and responsibility.

Recommendations

Educational risk factors ranging from grade retention to sexual harassment in school, pregnancy, and alcohol and drug abuse continue to affect girls and boys, as groups, at different rates and in different ways. We recommend that:

- Future policy interventions against risk factors such as teen pregnancy take into account the resiliency approach to risk that builds on the social and cultural resources that groups of students bring to school.
- The especially high dropout rate of Hispanic females be examined carefully, and dropout prevention programs target this group's strengths.
- All schools develop, implement, and strictly enforce sexual harassment policies. Sexual harassment affects a substantial number of boys and girls, although its effects appear more harmful for girls. By making schools unpleasant and unsafe for girls, harassment affects their educational success.
- Programs to diminish teen pregnancy or school violence, especially, should adopt an approach that involves all students—boys and girls—in the process of remedying these social problems.
- Researchers examine and explain further the different relationship for girls and boys between grade repetition and dropping out.

Extracurriculars:
Extras That Add Up

◆

The courses girls take and their performance in them constitute only one aspect of girls' school experience. Most
schools offer a variety of extracurricular activities, both to
connect students to their schools and to encourage skills and
development. This encouragement seems to have positive outcomes. Data from the 1992 National Education Longitudinal
Study (NELS) on high school seniors suggest an association
between attendance, academic achievement, educational aspirations, and extracurricular participation. Students involved
in extracurricular activities were "three times as likely to perform in the top quartile on a composite math and reading
assessment compared with non-participants."[1] Other research
corroborates the generally positive relationship between participation in extracurricular activities and school success.[2]

Just as boys' and girls' academic experience differs, so too
does their extracurricular experience. Data from the U.S.
Department of Education show more boys than girls participate in sports, especially team sports: Twice as many twelfth-
grade boys as girls take part in an interscholastic athletic team
sport or an interscholastic individual sport.[3]

Nonsports activities show the reverse pattern. More girls
than boys participate in the performing arts, school government and clubs, and literary activities. In 1992, 25 percent of
twelfth-grade girls played in the school band or orchestra compared to 15 percent of boys; 18 percent of girls were involved
in school government (compared to 13 percent of boys); 24

percent of girls spent time on the newspaper or yearbook (compared to 14 percent of boys). More girls (17 percent) than boys (10 percent) also cluster in school and community service.[4]

These numbers suggest that extracurricular choices reinforce traditional areas of gender competency rather than broaden girls' and boys' interests. In some respects, girls' extracurricular activities mirror the areas of engagement and competence evident in the formal curriculum.

Nearly all public school students have access to a "core of extracurricular activities," such as participation in sports, the yearbook, literary magazine, and school newspaper; band, orchestra, and chorus; booster clubs; school government; theater and dance; honor societies; and a wide range of interest-based clubs including science club, chess club, debate club, and chapters of groups such as the Future Teachers of America and 4-H.[5] Extracurricular activities often promote "teamwork, individual and group responsibility, physical strength and endurance, competition, diversity, and a sense of culture and community."[6] Community service, or "service learning," has recently become part of this set of experiences.

Sports

More girls are taking to the field each year—as they have since 1972— but the rate of increase is slowing: Girls' participation in sports rose only four percent from 1991-92 to 1996-97. In 1997, 1 in 3 girls took part in high school sports, compared with 1 in 2 boys. Participation rates are similar for girls from different racial and ethnic groups—a marked change from the past—although black girls are more likely than white girls to face transportation or funding problems. Socioeconomic status determines access more than race or ethnicity. Sports participation, in general, is linked not just to higher academic achievement but also to better physical and mental health and greater leadership capacity. Sports that confer high status, however, may hinder boys' identity development. Like classroom interactions, sports can either challenge or reinforce stereotypes about girls' and boys' roles. Stereotypes keep boys as well as girls from enjoying some athletic activities.

Sports receive by far the most attention of any extracurricular activities in schools, the research literature, and the media. High-profile boys' teams like football and basketball still command most of the spotlight. But as more and more girls have taken the field in the last 25 years, their teams have drawn notice, too. In the late 1990s major sportswear companies launched national ad campaigns featuring girls. The attention was overdue: The number of women and girls in athletics has risen between 1992 and 1998, yet in 1995, female sports received approximately 5 percent of the TV and print media sports coverage given to male sports.[7]

Table 18
Total Number of Participants in High School Sports

	1991–1992	1992–1993	1993–1994	1994–1995	1995–1996	1996–1997
Female	1,940,816	1,997,489	2,124,755	2,240,461	2,367,936	2,472,043
Male	3,429,855	3,416,389	3,478,530	3,536,359	3,634,359	3,706,225

Abridged from Women's Sports Facts (East Meadow, NY: The Women's Sports Foundation, 1997)

However, while advertisers' attention to female athletes is a welcome change, gains in girls' participation since 1992 have been unremarkable. Girls' participation in sports rose only four percent from 1991–92 to 1996–97.[8] (See Table 18.) This modest gain was in marked contrast to the nearly 600 percent increase measured from 1971 to 1992. In a 1997 "report card on gender equity" published by AAUW and other members of the National Coalition for Women and Girls in Education, athletics received a grade of only "C."[9] The publication marked the twenty-fifth anniversary of Title IX, the federal law prohibiting sex discrimination in education.

Girls' four percent participation gain since 1992 reflects a leveling off of the dramatic gains in girls' sports participation in schools between 1971 and 1992. In 1997, 1 in 3 girls took part in high school sports.[10] This number contrasts sharply with pre-Title IX figures: In 1971, the year Title IX was passed, only 1 in 27 girls took part in high school sports. Boys' participation rates have remained constant: 1 in 2 play sports in high school.[11] The cumulative outcome after twenty-five years of Title IX is that "more girls are participating in a wider array of physical activities and sports than ever before in American history."[12]

Girls from different racial and ethnic groups appear to participate in sports at similar rates. The Feminist Majority Foundation concluded that black and white girls participate equally in sports and fitness, although "black girls who quit sports are more likely [than white girls] to have problems with transportation or inadequate funds."[13] The equal participation of black and white girls in sports marks a significant improvement; earlier data reported that African American females represented less than 5 percent of all high school athletes.[14] Socioeconomic status, however, appears to limit girls' sports participation more than race or ethnicity. According to *The President's Council on Physical Fitness and Sports Report: Physical Activity and Sport in the Lives of Girls*, "poverty substantially limits many girls' access to physical activity and sport, especially girls of color who are overrepresented in lower socioeconomic groups."[15]

Table 19
Sports Programs, Ranked by Popularity (Numbers of Participants) by Gender, 1995–96

Female Students		Male Students	
Activity	**Participants**	**Activity**	**Participants**
Basketball	445,869	Football	957,573
Track & Field (Outdoor)	379,060	Basketball	545,596
Volleyball	357,576	Track & Field (Outdoor)	454,645
Softball (Fast Pitch)	305,217	Baseball	444,476
Soccer	209,287	Soccer	283,728
Tennis	146,573	Wrestling	221,162
Cross Country	140,187	Cross Country	168,203
Swimming & Diving	111,360	Golf	140,011
Field Hockey	56,142	Tennis	136,534
Golf	39,634	Swimming & Diving	81,000

Abridged from summary of The 1996 High School Athletics Participation Survey (Kansas City, MO: The National Federation of State High School Associations, 1996).

In high schools, basketball is the most popular sport for girls; more than 16,000 high schools (upwards of 80 percent) have girls' basketball teams.[16] A 1995-96 Athletics Participation Study found that boys and girls generally participate in the same sports, with roughly similar distribution among the sports. The top ten girls' programs, from the most popular down, were: basketball; track and field; volleyball; fast-pitch softball; soccer; tennis; cross country; swimming and diving; field hockey; and golf. Boys participated in baseball rather than fast-pitch softball; football rather than volleyball; and wrestling rather than field hockey.[17] As an extramural sport, soccer is popular with both sexes: In 1994 approximately 41 percent of players were girls and women.[18] (See Table 19.) Some school districts have established competitive girls' teams in traditionally male areas. Minnesota, for example, introduced girls' ice hockey in 1995; when the year ended, 80 percent of the female players planned to continue in the sport.[19]

Effects, Good and Bad

The effects of sports participation may vary for girls and boys. A longitudinal study of 209 high school juniors linked athletic team participation to "identity foreclosure"—in other words, stunted identity development—especially for boys. The authors conclude that "the high status afforded male athletes is detrimental to their overall psychological development."[20]

For girls, less likely to derive "consistent gains in status" from extracurricular activities including sports, participation may promote identity development, the study found. A study of gifted high school peer groups of girls in 1997 found that the girls' "involvement in activities valued by the school (athletics and the arts) leads to higher self-esteem, positive attitudes toward school, and less self-destructive behavior."[21]

These and other health benefits of sports for girls are well documented. Research consistently links participation in sports and physical activity with increased self-esteem and good physical and mental health, including lower rates of depression, cancer, and osteoporosis.[22] Further, high school girls who participate in team sports are 40 percent less likely to drop out of school, and 33 percent less likely to become pregnant.[23] They also are less likely to smoke cigarettes. As with other areas of school participation and achievement, timing is critical: Girls who are not involved in physical activity by age ten have only a 10 percent chance of being athletic when they are twenty-five.[24]

Evidence of academic benefits from sports is also growing. A recent study links sports participation to higher science achievement for white girls. In that study, Sandra Hanson and Rebecca Kraus examined 1980 and 1982 data on more than 20,000 high school students, noting students' attitudes toward science, the number of science courses taken, and performance on standardized tests. The research was controlled for factors including socioeconomic status and family influences. The study concluded that sports participation helped white girls develop the confidence and persistence needed to succeed in science courses. No such benefits were found for boys and African American girls. The authors hypothesized that black girls have the self-confidence needed to succeed in science without sports participation.[25]

Research has also identified several interesting secondary or collateral benefits for girls' sports participation. A 1997 Title IX report by the National Coalition for Girls and Women in Education found that 80 percent of female managers of Fortune 500 companies have a sports background.[26]

Making and Breaking Gender Stereotypes

The link between sports and leadership for girls undoubtedly derives in part from the unique capacities of school sports to prompt students and adults to question their own assumptions about gender. *Girls in the Middle*, a 1996 study published by the AAUW Educational Foundation, showed that "even though talk about gender" equity in a school may be "private and informal," sports, particularly in rural schools, "acts as an important, if unacknowledged, catalyst for discussion of gender and gender roles." Visible and culturally valued sports, especially in school districts without a prominent, policy-oriented discussion of gender equity, "offer adults an opportunity to challenge prevailing stereotypes ... and provide an opportunity [for girls] to ... critique 'ladylike' behavior." In one rural Southern school, for example, a teacher said of a female basketball player, "She is a cocky little thing." The basketball coach responded, "You have to have a certain confidence to play." This exchange broadened into a rich discussion of the faculty's mixed reactions to girls who seemed sure of themselves and were leaders among their peers.[27] Sports, in other words, because their gender stereotypes are readily apparent, have unique capacities to provoke students and educators to view masculinity and femininity in broader ways.

On the other hand, sports have equally powerful capacities to reinforce rigid gender conventions and roles. Ridicule, and the labels of "girl" or "sissy" assigned to boys who do not excel at or enjoy traditionally male sports, undoubtedly curtail boys' enthusiasm to pursue "female" athletic activities, such as skating, and may explain why data were not found for male participation in traditionally female sports.[28] Barrie Thorne finds that even young children ascribe gender differences to physical activities. When girls do not participate in "male" activities, such as soccer, their behavior is attributed to a lack of ability. When boys do not participate in "female" activities, such as hopscotch, their behavior is attributed to a lack of interest, based on the gendered nature of the activity.[29] Sports carry a clear set of assumptions: Only girls participate in some, and only boys participate in others. Those who cross the lines must be deviant in some way. As Jay Coakley writes,

> [Statements like this] are based on the assumption that "real" sports involve "manly" things like displays of aggression and physical dominance over others.[30] If sports involve not only these things, but grace, balance, and coordination, one or both of these things occur: The sports are demeaned, or the bodies of the athletes are sexualized and evaluated from top to bottom. In either case, the physical skills of the athletes are ignored and women athletes are trivialized.[31]

Because students "police" gender roles so obviously and rigorously in sports, the emergence of acclaimed and successful female athletes in the school context holds great potential to challenge stereotypes about body image, physical beauty, and girls' leadership and competitive skills. Those who expect girls to be deferential, modest, and immaculately groomed may be slow to accept girls as athletic competitors. But change is possible. In fact, there is clear evidence that women and men become fans of women's athletics when given the opportunity to learn about teams and players. According to the National

Council for Research on Women, "early reports suggest that the Women's National Basketball Association (WNBA) games exceed predictions of popularity and interest, and that girls are finding inspiration in female sports figures."[32] A 1997 report that measured progress on equity in areas affected by Title IX noted that 87 percent of parents now accept the idea that sports are equally important for boys and girls.[33]

Persistent Barriers to Girls

Despite manifest progress, research literature of the last five years cites a number of persistent barriers and disincentives to girls' sports participation. The Feminist Majority Foundation writes that "even girls who participate in sports and fitness cite obstacles, such as boys who refuse to pass balls to girls, or who criticize girls' performances; girls getting picked for teams after all the boys are picked; guy teachers who assume girls are not as good as boys; and better coaches and equipment for boys' teams."[34] This finding echoes research from 1992: Girls age 9–12 reported barriers such as "unfair treatment by the boys they were playing with, the assumption that they were not good players, inappropriate level of challenge, lack of opportunity, and time conflicts with other activities."[35]

A 1993 study found that picture books for young readers portray girls and women as sports participants much less frequently than males. According to the *Melpomene Journal*, out of 105 books surveyed, only twenty-eight encouraged girls to participate in sports.[36] The diminishing number of female coaches compounds the problem of limited role models.[37] And a number of studies have found that the "erroneous but long-standing belief that physically active girls are more likely to become lesbians" serves to "intimidate and silence" women who complain about "gender injustice in sports."[38]

In addition, schools have done little to encourage girls to exercise, cutting physical education requirements instead. In 1995 only a little more than half (57 percent) of the nation's ninth- through twelfth-grade girls took school classes in physical education, and only about one-fourth (24 percent) took these classes daily. Only 52 percent of all high school girls surveyed said they exercised vigorously three or more times in the previous week, compared with 74 percent of boys.[39]

Following a zero-sum game model, girls' sports are also still viewed as a threat to male sports. In 1996, acting in response to a 1992 U.S. Supreme Court ruling that upheld the right of girls and women to sue institutions for financial damages in cases of discrimination, Congress suggested that new rules were needed to protect current funding for the most traditional of all sports: football.[40]

Despite concerns that Title IX enforcement will "gut" such popular, overwhelminglyly male sports, it is important to recognize that the law does not mandate numerical quotas, statistical balancing, or even equal spending for boys and girls. Instead, it stipulates that schools provide athletic opportunities to female and males substantially proportionate to their respective enrollments and that they expand programs for the gender that is underrepresented.[41] Generating opportunities for female athletes has meant allocating resources toward historically less popular athletics, but as a result, these sports have become more popular, as evidenced by the WNBA, and more enthusiastically pursued by female students. The progress made toward gender equity in sports since the passage of Title IX in 1972 provides a striking example of how attitudes toward gender roles and competencies can change when schools distribute resources in an equitable manner.

In short, sports are a celebrated part of the implicit curriculum in many schools, although they are formally separated from academic activities. Through sports, students absorb a number of lessons about popularity, physical skills, leadership abilities, camaraderie, and teamwork. Research and other literature of the last five years attribute an array of direct and indirect benefits to sports participation. Like classroom interactions, sports can either redefine or reinforce traditional views about girls' and boys' roles. Given sports' visibility in our culture, it is important that the schools strive to equalize girls' and boys' access to sports and see that both groups can win acclaim for their sports prowess. As girls' participation in sports increases, schools need to hire more female coaches and administrators and accord girls' sports the same social value as boys' teams, so that girls are not left cheering for the boys, with no one to cheer for them.

◆　◆　◆

Other Extracurricular Activities

Extracurricular activities outside of sports also promote academic achievement for girls and boys, both black and white. Just as with sports, socioeconomic status (SES) appears more important than gender or race in determining participation. Participation rates for low-SES students are lower for all activities except vocational and professional clubs. Here, low-SES students are almost twice as likely to take part. Such data suggest that many schools may informally track extracurricular activities just as they track academic classes. Just as sports offer girls a chance to learn competitive and leadership skills commonly thought of as "male," service learning may offer boys an opportunity to practice social skills, such as social skills, communication, and community interest, more typically assigned to girls.

In the graduating class of 1992, 80 percent of seniors reported taking part in at least one non-athletic extracurricular activity.[42] The data are not reported by gender and activity, making it impossible to differentiate between activities in which girls or boys participate. However, data do illustrate that female seniors consistently participate more often in academic clubs, honorary societies, student government, newspaper, or yearbook.[43] Similarly, data are not available by both race and gender—a consistent difficulty throughout this research. However, examinations of race data alone indicate that Asian American seniors participated more in academic clubs and honorary societies, while black seniors participated more in student government. White seniors participated most in newspaper or yearbook activities.[44]

Although Jose Cardenas and Myra Sadker et al. found that females as a group continue to be excluded from extracurricular activities, socioeconomic status, rather than gender or race, may be the key variable predicting students' participation in extracurricular activities, as appears to be the case in athletics.[45] Students from lower socioeconomic status (SES) backgrounds are less likely to participate (75 percent) than are high-SES students (87 percent). Participation rates for low-SES students were consistently lower in all areas except, notably, vocational or professional clubs. In these activities alone, low-SES students are almost two times as likely to participate.[46] These data suggest that extracurricular activities, like curricular activities, may be informally tracked in many schools. (See Chapter 1.)

Like sports, extracurricular activities in general are linked with higher student achievement and identification with the schools. In a recent study, Alan Shoho and Irene Petrisky found significantly lower levels of alienation in students who took part in extracurricular activities.[47] The amount of participation in extracurricular activities also has been positively related to academic achievement for both black and white students.[48]

Service Learning

Among non-athletic extracurricular activities, service learning provides the most explicit bridge to curricular areas. Philosophically rooted in the role of schools as developers of character and, as John Dewey imagined, places where students learn the art of democratic citizenship, service learning is essentially student volunteerism either on- or off-campus.[49] In some states (for example, Kentucky), graduation requirements emphasize application and integration of skills; service learning fills this requirement.[50] Like other forms of extracurricular activities, service learning produces benefits for students. Miranda Yates and James Youniss link service learning to identity development; Pat Hutchinson and Tom Hughes suggest that service learning makes meaningful learning fun; and Alan Haskitz presents a validated model that links service learning with enhanced academic performance.[51] Further, Jennifer Ocif and Beverly Marshall-Goodell suggest that service learning can be combined with mentoring, known to be beneficial for engaging girls.[52]

It is not yet clear to what extent service learning has become a component of education; also unknown is whether girls and boys participate at different rates. However, just as sports offer girls an opportunity to master skills and traits typically assigned to males—competition, leadership, camaraderie, and same-sex friendships—service learning, with its emphasis on social outreach and civic responsibility, affords boys a parallel opportunity. Through service learning, boys can develop traits historically assigned to females—social concern, community interest, and the ability to interact across social worlds.

Another extracurricular activity not sponsored by schools and often not endorsed by them is student employment. Much of the research on students' paid employment—typically focusing on middle-class students—has emphasized the negative outcomes of work, as it competes for an adolescent's school study time.[53] For students in poorer neighborhoods, however, paid employment appears tied to better school performance. A 1996 study of the adolescent working poor in Harlem found that:

> when we look at the experience of the working youth in this [context], we see a very impressive degree of engagement in school when compared against those they consider their peers in their neighborhoods, many of whom have dropped out and can no longer even find minimum-wage employment. For many of the young people we interviewed, the confrontation with low-wage work made clear in concrete ways what a lifetime of secondary labor market employment would mean—poor wages, few chances for advancement, minimal respect, and declining prospects for independent adult living. The experience spurred them on to further training as an avenue of escape from this end of the labor market.[54]

The study concludes that for poor urban teenagers, "aspirations for more valuable credentials often develop as a result of work experience."

Paid work might have particular benefits for teen girls: The study concluded: "[Out of wedlock pregnancy] is far less likely to happen when young women work." The study urges more ethnographic work to test the hypothesis that "early and sustained work experience may well be part of the answer to cutting back on teen pregnancy."[55]

Summary

Extracurricular activities enrich the lives of girls and boys, building self-esteem, leadership, and social skills; improving general health; challenging gender stereotypes; and even, perhaps, boosting academic performance. Students involved in

3 6

extracurricular activities are likelier than their peers to score high on math and reading tests. For white girls, sports participation appears linked to higher science achievement; no such benefits were found for boys and black girls.

Overall, girls' and boys' participation patterns in extracurricular activities send a troubling message. Twice as many boys as girls take part in team sports or interscholastic individual sports. Despite significant progress since the 1972 enactment of Title IX, girls continue to face barriers to participation in school sports. In 1997, 1 in 3 girls took part in high school sports, compared with 1 in 2 boys.

In other extracurricular activities, particularly in the performing arts, school government, and literary activities, girls outnumber boys. The distinctive patterns suggest that extracurricular choices reinforce traditional areas of gender competency rather than broaden boys' and girls' interests.

The biggest barrier to participation in sports as well as other extracurricular activities appear to be posed not by gender or race, but by socioeconomic status. SES is still the key variable in predicting student participation, with low-SES students less likely to take part. The development of "service learning" has the potential to broaden boys' attitudes about the socially acceptable roles open to them, just as the opening of sports to girls has changed girls' views about what is acceptable feminine behavior.

Recommendations

- Girls' sports participation is a school success story. Girls' involvement in sports has shown extraordinary growth since the enactment of Title IX—the federal law prohibiting sex discrimination in education—in 1972. Recently we have seen a plateauing of these gains. Schools should be required to comply with Title IX so that we do not slip back on important gains. School districts must be vigilant in enforcing Title IX.
- School districts and schools should aggressively continue to develop, recruit, and hire female coaches to serve as female role models.

- Specific procedures need to be put in place to track enforcement of Title IX in grades K–12. Data collection and disclosure need to be mandatory for school districts by state.
- Economics appears to be a bigger barrier than gender to participation in extracurricular activities. Given the demonstrated collateral benefits of extracurricular activities such as sports to girls' academic achievement and esteem, schools need to address more aggressively the socioeconomic barriers and other factors that limit student participation. Schools should structure extracurricular activities at times when they do not interfere with employment opportunities. Attempts should be made to work with employers in local communities to see how extracurricular and work experiences can be linked.
- Schools should consider boys' underrepresentation in honor societies and literary extracurricular activities as a problem of equity. These activities perhaps contribute to girls' advantages in writing, reading interpretation, and verbal skills. Schools should work with parents and counselors to encourage and direct boys into extracurricular opportunities that can expand and enrich their cognitive and developmental growth. These extracurricular activities should be portrayed as being relevant for both sexes.

CHAPTER SIX

INFLUENCING STUDENT CAREER CHOICES

◆

Inequity exists to the extent that girls contemplate and pursue a narrower set of career opportunities than do boys, as the research has found.[1] This inequity reverberates beyond school and into the labor force, where only six percent of women are in careers categorized as "nontraditional."[2] In fact, women cluster in only 20 of the more than 400 job categories, and two out of three minimum-wage earners are women.[3]

Job projections for the 21st-century economy leave no room for an education system that in the 1990s is still condoning limits on gender roles. Economists predict that by the year 2000, 65 percent of all jobs will require technical skills, 20 percent will be professional, while only 15 percent will rely on unskilled labor.[4] Consequently, college and advanced degrees are becoming more the norm than the exception. In order to meet the higher demands of tomorrow's workplace, today's students need to gain not only a different knowledge base than past generations of students, but also the ability to adapt to rapid changes, renew their skills, educate themselves throughout their lives, and understand the increasingly vital connection between education and work.

Anne Chapman's chart (see page 86) underscores the importance of resisting rigid definitions of "masculine" and "feminine" roles in school.[5] Rigid gender-role definitions create barriers for both boys and girls by minimizing the importance of certain "skill-sets" and values for each group. As Chapman's chart shows, boys can no longer afford to shun the communi-

GENDER ROLES

A girl graduating from high school in the next few years will face ...	A boy graduating from high school in the next few years will face ...
♦ the absolute certainty of encountering situations in which being aggressive and competitive are to her advantage.	♦ the absolute certainty of encountering situations in which being aggressive and competitive are damaging to him.
♦ the virtual certainty of working for pay outside the home for decades of her adult life.	♦ the virtual certainty of being married to a woman who works for pay outside the home during most of their married life.
♦ the virtual certainty that she will be called upon, in the course of her working life, to exercise skills and attitudes that have been traditionally considered "masculine."	♦ the virtual certainty of being called upon, in the course of his working life, to exercise skills and attitudes traditionally considered "feminine."
♦ the strong probability of divorce.	♦ the strong probability of divorce.
♦ the virtual certainty that, if she is divorced and has children, she will be the custodial single parent with major financial responsibility for herself and her children.	♦ the strong probability, if divorced with children, of remarrying and having to contribute to the emotional, as well as the financial, well-being of two sets of offspring; and the small, but increasing, probability that he will be the sole custodial single parent.
♦ the strong probability of conflict between career and family obligations.	♦ the strong probability of conflict between career and family obligations.
♦ the strong possibility of being sexually harassed on the job.	♦ the small but not insignificant possibility of being sexually harassed on the job.
♦ the increasing possibility of earning more money than her husband.	♦ the increasing probability of having a wife who earns more than he does.

Source: Anne Chapman, *A Great Balancing Act* (Washington, DC: National Association of Independent Schools, 1997)

cation skills needed to function in an information-driven economy any more than girls can afford to bypass managerial and technical skills important to the professional fields projected to boom in the 21st century. A more balanced occupational distribution hinges on our applying these lessons.

Over the years, the federal government has acted to correct the lopsided occupational distribution of male and female workers. In 1993-94 the U.S. Department of Education called on Congress to amend the 20-year-old Women's Educational Equity Act (WEEA) program to incorporate "school-to-work transition programs, guidance and counseling activities, and other programs to increase opportunities for women and girls to enter a technologically demanding workplace and, in particular, to enter highly skilled, high-paying careers in which women and girls have been underrepresented."[6]

Career exploration and preparation present particularly difficult challenges to the goal of equitable—and excellent—education. Schools' failure to counter assumptions about appropriate occupational roles for girls and boys tends to affirm those assumptions. Even when boys and girls receive "equal" treatment in career preparation, counseling, and programs, the absence of a conscious effort to challenge their learned beliefs about possible occupations for their gender leads to inequitable distributions in occupational fields.

Schools, of course, cannot singlehandedly change assumptions about gender roles and careers. However, they do provide much of the information students receive about careers through formal mechanisms such as counseling and tracking, and through informal but no less powerful cues such as Career Day, bulletin board displays, guest speakers, and assemblies. Schools can play a pivotal role in either reinforcing or challenging gendered assumptions about career options through these same formal mechanisms. This chapter explores some ways in which girls' choices, in particular, are curtailed and some of the interventions that might widen their opportunities.

◆　◆　◆

School to Work

Early data suggest that School-to-Work programs, begun in 1994, are not achieving their goal of correcting a sexually lopsided occupational distribution by encouraging girls and boys to pursue nontraditional careers. In School-to-Work initiatives, as in academic standards, rhetorical attention to helping "all students" succeed sometimes masks the needs of historically disadvantaged groups, including, in this case, girls.

School-to-Work programs, in which students practice skills valued in today's economy, including communication, group problem-solving, and data analysis, have great potential to broaden girls' sense of their career options and choices.[7] The School-to-Work Opportunities Act of 1994 seeks to ensure that all students are prepared for the work force and that they are able to see the connection between school-based learning and work-based applications. In concept, the initiative differs from vocational education in at least one key respect: School to Work is a broader effort designed to cover all students, including those bound for postsecondary education.

School to Work also addresses gender explicitly. The initiative aspires to "increase opportunities for minorities, women, and individuals with disabilities, by enabling individuals to prepare for careers that are not traditional for their race, gender, or disability."[8]

Have School-to-Work programs succeeded in this goal? It's too soon to tell for sure. Because of the law's recent inception, few data are available on current School-to-Work program participation rates by gender. A national assessment of School-to-Work participation rates, progress in meeting state goals to increase opportunities for young women in nontraditional employment, and other outcomes will first report results in fall 1998.[9]

Several recently released studies, however, have examined the performance of School to Work, particularly in its demonstration phase. Early data indicate that, unless changes are made, School to Work is not likely to provide many opportunities for girls or boys to enter or explore opportunities in nontraditional fields. Mary Wiberg writes that "almost no

What Happened to Vocational Education?

1992 goal: *Continued attention to gender equity in vocational education programs must be a high priority at every level of educational governance and administration.* (How Schools Shortchange Girls, page 86)

Analysis: *Vocational education in essence repeated the pattern found in science and mathematics. Students were tracked into vocational education courses according to gender stereotypes, and research recognized a lack of nontraditional role models. The 1990 amendments to the Carl C. Perkins Vocational Education Act of 1984 mandated that each state set aside 10.5 percent of Perkins funds for two sex equity programs: one to eliminate bias in vocational education and another to assist single mothers.*

1998 reality: *Assessing the impact of vocational education set asides on women's wages is difficult because many positive outcomes are not apparent until months or years after a program's completion. A 1995 evaluation of vocational equity programs found significant salary increases for displaced homemakers and single parents who took part in Perkins-funded vocational education programs in nine states.* A 1994 assessment of Perkins Act set asides found large funding effects at the secondary education level, where on average, funded districts offered twice as many services as unfunded districts.***

continued . . .

attention has been paid to the issues related to the participation of all students in the system ... many policymakers and planners do not consider equity and access priorities."[10] Donna Milgram and Kristin Watkins similarly discovered that:

Of the 14 regular demonstration sites, three had no young women and three had only one or two young women. Over 90 percent of young women clustered in five demonstration sites where the occupational areas were traditional for their gender—allied health careers, teaching and education, graphic arts, and office technology. Even when a fifteenth, nontraditional site was included, only 16 percent (41 women) [of the women in all the sites] were in nontraditional skills training; almost half (20) of them were in the single nontraditional site.[11]

Sue Rosser and Charlotte Hogsett note that Washington, the only state to invest substantial state dollars in School to Work, has no specific focus on gender: "Although the Final Report to the Governor constantly repeats that School to Work is for ALL [original emphasis] students, gender is referred to only once in the entire document."[12] This is particularly disconcerting, since Washington's materials will likely be used to guide other states.[13]

The *Study of School to Work Initiatives* and *Home Grown Progress:*

The Evolution of Innovative School to Work Programs also evaluate School to Work's early performance.[14] The *Study of School to Work Initiatives* did not examine gender equity but recommended further research concerning "access and equity of School-to-Work programs: studies of student tracking, equal educational and occupational opportunity, and sex role and racial stereotyping."[15] *Home Grown Progress*, which reviewed sixteen School-to-Work programs, concluded that:

. . . continued from previous page

The report notes that *"except where Perkins funds are available, few counselors are actually trained to deal specifically with the vocational needs"* of nontraditional students and single parents.***

Sources:
* Empowering America's Families: Documenting the Success of Vocational Equity Programs for Women and Girls *(Washington, DC: National Coalition for Women and Girls in Education, March 1995: 1-5.*
** *U.S. Department of Education, Office of Research, National Assessment of Vocational Education, Final Report to Congress, V. v IV, 1994.*
*** *Ibid., p. 51.*

the occupational focus of school-to-work programs is a major factor in determining the balance of male and female students. In particular, the youth apprenticeship programs have increased the percentage of females participating, largely by adding new occupational areas—such as health and business/finance—to their traditionally male-oriented occupational programs (such as printing and metal working). For these programs, efforts to recruit males and females to programs focused on occupational areas traditionally dominated by the other gender have not yielded better male-to-female balances by themselves.[16]

Lynn Olson, author of a major overview of School-to-Work initiatives, agrees. She

saw more evidence of gender differentiation among programs ... girls tended to cluster in health care and business programs; boys tended to dominate—almost to the point of exclusion—in many industrial and engineering programs. This seemed to stem less from discrimination on the part of the initiatives, many of which were actively trying to recruit both sexes, than from stereotypes within society at large. A few places, such as Procter & Gamble Co., had managed to surmount these preconceptions and recruit nearly

1. Today, 62 million women age 16 and over comprise ____% of the total U.S. labor force.

a. 25%   b. 33%   c. 46%   d. 53%

2. Women high school graduates (with no college) working year-round full time earned, on average, $21,298. Fully employed men who completed 9th to 12th grade (no high school diploma) earned, on average, $_____

a. $15,553   b. $18,939
c. $21,950   d. $23,994

3. In 1995, 21.8 million adults (persons 18 years of age and over) had incomes below the poverty level. Women represented _____% of all persons 18 years of age and over who had incomes below poverty level.

a. 50%   b. 70%   c. 80%   d. 90%

4. Between now and the year 2000 the number of women entering the work force is expected to increase. The most significant increase is expected to be among Hispanic women. Their work force participation is projected to reach 6.8 million, an increase of _____% since 1994.

a. 25%   b. 33%   c. 45%   d. 66%

Sources:

Excerpted from Labor Force Quiz, U.S. Department of Labor, Women's Bureau, 1996. [Answers: 1-c; 2-d; 3-b; 4-b]

as many young women as young men.[17]

In School-to-Work initiatives, rhetorical attention to the fortunes of *all* students sometimes discourages nontraditional career exploration by historically disadvantaged groups. Jenny Erwin relates the following incident:

The state gender equity administrator pointed out that providing funding for the needs of teen parents—child care, transportation, and so on—was important. A team member turned to her and said, "The School-to-Work Opportunities Act is not a special populations bill. It's to serve *all* students." To which she responded "Well, we're redefining *all* students." Unfortunately, this story is not an isolated incident. One colleague told me that we didn't have to deal with that equity stuff any more. School to Work was to serve all students![18]

Further research will determine whether School to Work, as it matures, makes a concerted effort toward gender equity (for example, through identification of exemplary gender equitable programs). To their credit, states have made some efforts to broaden students' sense of "plausible" occupations. Iowa reports that it uses "mentors as nontraditional role models for females," and Oklahoma reports that it provides "career awareness and development, counseling, pilot programs, outreach and awareness activities, student recruitment, marketing, and supportive services [to target] young women for nontraditional careers.[19]

However, available data indicate that girls are still pursuing traditional occupations, while boys are avoiding fields like nursing, which would be nontraditional for them. Clearly, School to Work has tremendous potential for gender equity, but unless monitored is unlikely to achieve equitable results for either girls or boys. Instead, it risks becoming a missed powerful opportunity to actively transform students' career preparation and aspiration along more gender-equitable lines.

Career "Choices"

Too many students make career choices in an information vacuum. Left to their own devices, girls and boys tend to self-select into fields traditional for their gender: Girls cluster in social sciences, health services, and education; boys gravitate disproportionately toward engineering and business. School counselors and mentors exert extraordinary influence in students' career decisions—but often manage such heavy caseloads that time for meaningful interaction with students is limited.

Career development theorists identify career exploration as a stage that typically occurs during adolescence, when boys and girls try out various roles in part-time work, volunteer work, or in school/community activities.[20] Career exploratory behavior is the initial stage of career choice and is characterized by a desire to acquire knowledge about the self (through assessment of abilities, interests, values, and needs) and the work world in order to make an informed decision. As *How Schools Shortchange Girls* recommended in 1992, teachers and counselors can take the lead in encouraging girls and boys to explore all of their options, however nontraditional. Counselors acknowledge that "students must be made aware of and understand all their options if they are to make informed decisions."[21]

However, data on the intended majors of college-bound students gathered on the SAT and ACT student descriptive surveys tell another story—that of the self-selection of high school boys and girls, as populations, into fields conventional for their gender.[22] As Table 20 illustrates, a larger proportion of female than male SAT takers intended to major in visual and performing arts, biological sciences, education, foreign or classical languages, health and allied services, language and literature, and the social sciences. A larger proportion of male than female SAT takers intended to major in agriculture and natural resources, business and commerce, engineering, mathematics, physical sciences, and other areas.

What have schools done since 1992 to encourage male and female students to venture from the "path of least resistance" in their career choices? Educational reform initiatives such as School to Work and the Women's Educational Equity Act (WEEA), and laws such as Title IX, have led counselors and

Table 20
Percentage of Intended College Majors (SAT Takers)

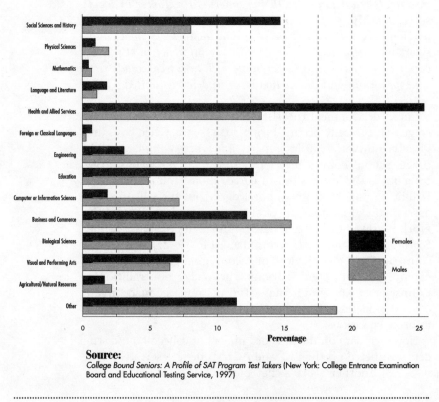

Source:
College Bound Seniors: A Profile of SAT Program Test Takers (New York: College Entrance Examination Board and Educational Testing Service, 1997)

GENDER GAPS: WHERE SCHOOLS STILL FAIL OUR CHILDREN

teachers alike to question biases, assumptions, and stereotypes about student ability and career expectations, and to encourage students to explore nontraditional avenues.

Counselors and mentors possess extraordinary potential to influence students' career choices. Karen Arnold's 1994 research on high school valedictorians concludes, alarmingly, that individual "academic achievement reduces gender and social class differences in career outcomes only when professionally related undergraduate experiences," including exposure to mentors and counseling, "overcome circumscribed views of the occupational world."[23] In a 1990 study Ofra Nevo discovered that students rated discussions with their counselors as more important than objective tests, interests inventories, or vocational information in making career choices.[24] Yet high student-to-counselor ratios often impede meaningful interaction: Sometimes a single counselor is responsible for as many as 300 students. In addition, counselors have other responsibilities besides helping students make informed decisions about their futures.[25]

Counselors sometimes help students explore their career interests through standard inventories and surveys. Students use inventories to assess their strengths and weaknesses in particular areas, and then match their strengths with potential careers. Unfortunately, these often-outdated tools may reinforce many of the biases that young women encounter. Helen Farmer notes, "Since evidence of gender differences continue to be found for career interest measures, it seems imperative to revive the NIE [1975 National Institute of Education] Guidelines orienting women clients to the effects of their socialization on their scores."[26] Despite the many programs and guidelines devoted to reducing bias and efforts by counselors, the media, and others involved in education, occupational sex-role socialization still pervades and inhibits the career exploration process.[27]

Research illustrates that teachers' attitudes, methods of teaching, and their classroom atmosphere also affect girls and their enthusiasm for nontraditional fields.[28] In technology education, for example, stereotypes about appropriate careers for girls, a dearth of female role models, and a lack of basic career information in the classes dampened girls' interest in technology-based careers.[29]

Data are becoming available about high success rates in many career intervention programs. Rosser and Hogsett cite the Manufacturing Technology Partnership (MTP) program as one success story. During the 1993-94 school year, nearly 50 percent of those applying and nearly 45 percent of those accepted were female.[30] Successful elements of the program include female role models, "sexual harassment workshops, access to female mentors, emphasis on incentives for employers to recruit women for nontraditional careers, and training for counselors, principals, teachers and parents."[31]

Other studies have found that a focus on training young women for nontraditional careers yields success.[32] Patricia Campbell and Karen Steinbrueck report on more promising programs, in particular, Expanding Your Horizons in Science and Mathematics, which combines role models, hands-on science activities, and information on science careers during one-day conferences for middle school girls.[33]

Summary

Merely presenting career options to girls and boys is not enough to change learned behaviors and attitudes. Offering girls and boys "the same" career training opportunities without challenging stereotypes of gender-appropriate work does not advance an equitable career selection process, in which background variables such as gender do not exert a disproportionate influence on career choices.

School-to-Work programs, begun in 1994, illustrate this point. While data analysis on the programs won't be complete until fall 1998, early data suggest that the programs are not achieving their goal of correcting a sexually lopsided occupational distribution by encouraging girls and boys to pursue nontraditional careers. In School-to-Work initiatives, rhetorical attention to helping *all* students succeed sometimes masks the needs of historically disadvantaged groups, including, in this case, girls.

Partly because of their workloads, school counselors and mentors also frequently fail to help students make informed career decisions. Left to their own devices, girls and boys tend to self-select into fields traditional for their gender: Girls cluster in social sciences, health services, and education; boys gravitate disproportionately toward engineering and business. With caseloads of up to 300 students, school counselors are often hard-pressed to carry on meaningful interaction with students.

To encourage both boys and girls to explore a wide range of career opportunities, including those traditionally pursued by members of the other sex, career exploration programs must acknowledge and address influences such as cultural expectations and gender-role stereotypes, mathematics and science stereotypes, self-concept, self-esteem, fear of success, family and life planning, the role of parents and peers, and support systems.[34] Facing these pressures will help all students achieve financial independence and narrow the wage gap.

Girls themselves are re-envisioning their futures. In *Between Voice and Silence*, Jill Taylor, Carol Gilligan, and Amy Sullivan write that:

> The girls' hopes and plans—spoken about by some with the optimism of adolescence—often contradict society's general assumptions about how "at-risk" girls think about the future. These assumptions are rife with stereotypes that go something like this: these girls have little motivation or desire for achievement; rather than making plans for the future, they are present oriented; they may even be expecting a future in which public assistance plays a role. They have an external locus of control and are easy prey to negative influences from peers. ... The future the adolescent girls in the study envision for themselves differs from these stereotypes. Across racial and ethnic groups, with few exceptions, they express a strong preference for establishing themselves in a job or a career before making commitments to relationships with spouses, partners, or children.[35]

◆ ◆ ◆

Recommendations

- Evaluations of School-to-Work initiatives slated for 1999 should disaggregate data by sex to chart students' participation in nontraditional fields.
- If School-to-Work partnerships that integrate the formal school curriculum with "real-life" occupational experience continue to grow, they should focus on recruiting nontraditional students into sex-stereotyped professions such as nursing or business and finance. Simply offering students career options on paper without an understanding of the social incentives or disincentives for participation cannot be expected to alter students' sometimes limited notions of what a career "appropriate" for their gender might be.
- The School-to-Work initiative at the federal level should identify, replicate, and promote model programs—including internships, externships, and apprenticeships—that encourage nontraditional career exploration for boys and girls.
- Career development processes, orchestrated by counselors or mentors, should be established to help students identify traditional and nontraditional career options, understand occupational trend projections for high-wage and high-skilled careers, and develop individual educational and career plans.
- School to Work is more than internships and formal partnerships. All teachers should be aware of the occupational and social relevance of the knowledge, skills, and content they teach. They should be able to make specific links between "real world" applications and the formal curriculum.
- Researchers should investigate how and what girls, especially, know about economic trends and about the relationship between curriculum, course-taking choices, and occupational options. Such information must be made available to them.

CHAPTER SEVEN

....

Monitoring Gender Equity
in the 21st Century

◆

This report has revisited areas of historic concern for those interested in equity—math and science enrollment, tests and assessment, textbooks, and classroom interaction, among others. Emerging and developing educational trends, however, are more difficult to measure at present. This section describes briefly some educational trends that should be monitored for possible gender disparities in the next decade, which may develop even as familiar gender gaps diminish.

Demographic Changes: Differences Among Girls

This report has documented progress for girls as a whole, yet has also noted, to the extent possible, some differences among girls according to race, ethnicity, and class. Given projections about demographic changes in the 21st century, these differences in performance among groups of girls—often masked under general data that compares "girls" to "boys"—threaten to become more extreme and profound in consequence.

The Growth of the Hispanic Population

The Hispanic population, projected to reach 59 million by 2030, will become the largest racial/ethnic group in the United States. It is crucial that girls in this population receive an education that doesn't limit them to unskilled, subsistence, and seasonal or contingent jobs. Public education in the United States historically has supported the ideals of mobility and aspiration for minority and immigrant groups. Yet K–12 education to date apparently has not served the Hispanic population well. The Hispanic dropout rate hovers around 30 percent, prompting a 1998 Department of Education report, *No More Excuses*, to recommend $100 million in dropout prevention programs targeted to Hispanics. Soberingly, the dropout rate is worse among second-generation students than those newly arrived, suggesting that the problem becomes more rather than less pronounced the longer families have been in the country, and is not exclusively a function of non-English speaking status.[1]

Hispanic girls face unique struggles and risks, both in relation to white and African American girls and in relation to their male peers. The dropout rate for Hispanic females age 16 to 24 reached 30 percent in 1995, and the Hispanic teen pregnancy and birth rates have not followed the decline of white and African American rates. Furthermore, as Hispanic educators note, "the Latino culture values education ... but values family above all. And when it comes to choosing between going to school and helping the family, the family will win." Another Hispanic professor notes that the "greatest discrepancy between Hispanic and non-Hispanic white seniors has to do with the compatibility of students' home life with schooling." This incompatibility has especially powerful effects on some academically ambitious Hispanic girls who, according to scholar Rosa Maria Gil, when "faced with an American culture that promotes independence, self-fulfillment, and assertiveness," can "easily become overwhelmed by stress, conflict, and guilt." By the same token, however, high-achieving Hispanic females in academia routinely cite the resources of "family, language, and culture," and "family support" as critical to their success.[2]

Immigration and the Education of New American Girls

Immigration, especially from Asia and Mexico, will contribute substantially to the public school enrollment "boomlet" in the next decades. A few reports from 1998 support the argument that the children of immigrants do better in school than other American children. Yet schools are ill-prepared to cultivate the strengths and potential of this growing student population.

Although some districts in Florida, Texas, and California already have sizable immigrant populations (leading to the phenomenon of "majority-minority" schools), it is too early to tell what unique challenges and opportunities this public school influx will create for gender equity goals. Clearly, gender expectations and cultural norms among a white, middle-class American population differ in some respects from those upheld in other cultures. For example, a high-achieving female student in a 1998 study of immigration and San Diego's schools observed, "Hmong girls are expected to marry young and so are discouraged from pursuing education much beyond high school." Although this is not an expectation currently relevant to most native-born American girls, policymakers and researchers will have to confront a more complex array of gender values and cultures as the century progresses.

The National Center for Immigrant Students describes that in school, "immigrant girls ... encounter U.S. stereotypes of females. ... In their families, they also cope with powerful stereotypes" from their birth culture. A rise in female teen suicides, female gangs, and illicit drug commerce in immigrant communities attest to the cultural strains placed on this population of girls, in particular. The center notes further that terms such as "self-esteem" and "leadership" development, staples of American gender equity conversations, may have radically different meanings or contexts for immigrant girls.[3]

Regional Differences Among Girls

Control over education and the allocation of education dollars has been shifting steadily toward the states and away from the federal government. Consequently, differences in outcome among girls by region may become more acute in the coming century. For example, the Southern Regional Education Board (SREB) reported in 1998 a substantial gender gap on 1996 NAEP math scores in the Southern states. Girls in rural Southern regions perform at a lower level in mathematics and science than other girls across the country, and consistently below Southern region boys. The largest female achievement gap occurs between girls who live in rural areas of the Southern region states and rural girls elsewhere in the country. The gap is not seen in comparable rural, low-income sectors of other regions. While the SREB could not explain the gender gap, the gap's existence suggests that regional differences between girls may increase, despite an *overall* leveling off of gender differences in test performance nationwide.[4]

What to Watch: As girls as a whole move toward parity with boys in enrollment, performance, and educational opportunities, it will be critical to monitor subgroups of girls for significant discrepancies in their opportunities and performance. Gaps among girls based on racial, ethnic, economic, and regional differences may become more pronounced, even as the gaps between boys and girls in the aggregate diminish. These differences in educational outcomes must be monitored closely, particularly as demographic trends reconfigure the public school population.

Careers and New Fields of Knowledge

Historically, gender equity scholars have measured progress by the number of math and science courses girls take in high school, together with their enrollment in physics and the college "gatekeeper" courses of algebra and geometry. These courses are important, but economic projections about job growth also recommend girls' timely enrollment in specific kinds of math, science, and computer classes. If girls are to achieve economic independence and participate in cutting-edge fields of knowledge, more of them need to prepare for jobs in fields likely to create interesting and well-paid positions, at various skill levels, in the next century.

Boys, similarly, should recognize that as technologies become more complex, the need will increase for effective communicators across disciplines and cultures.

Computer Science

Aside from technology magnet schools, most public schools have limited offerings in computer science, programming, and applications. However, as this report shows, course enrollment to date in computer science electives and AP courses warn of an emerging gender gap in courses related to one of the boom industries of the next century. Computer science and applications electives attract very few girls, and in 1996 females comprised only 17 percent of AP computer science test takers. Meanwhile, computer companies face such a shortage of "tech talent" that some have begun to recruit high school students (predominantly male) with computer programming, graphics, and web design skills to fill gaps in their employee roster. Some of these students, the *Washington Post* recently reported, make as much as $50,000 a year for working three days a week. "In today's market," explained one high tech employer, "it's impossible to find someone with [advanced graphics computer] skills. The next ad I run may be in a high school newspaper."[5]

To solve the problem, corporations such as Microsoft and Novell have established certification programs in hundreds of high schools nationwide; teaching students how to design, build, and maintain computer networks. Although some have criticized the programs for shrewdly producing students to fill specific corporate needs, the better-designed programs do equip students for lucrative entry-level jobs, and prepare them for postsecondary computer science education. However controversial the certification programs, it is crucial that girls not get left behind in this field through underrepresentation in computer science and advanced mathematics classes. College computer science departments typically recommend, for admission to their often-competitive major, a high school preparation that includes four years of mathematics—including two years of algebra and analytic geometry—as well as relevant computer science classes, where possible.[6]

Biotechnology

An interdisciplinary science and technology field that encompasses genetic engineering, gene therapeutics, and pharmaceutical research, biotechnology has developed into a major growth industry over the last decade, and has fostered some of the most innovative scientific breakthroughs and lines of inquiry. Girls potentially interested in the field, however, can find themselves lagging in the "pipeline" without a sequence of high school courses. As recent research on women's math and science attrition points out, "although collegiate interventions" can promote higher female enrollment, "the critical damage is done much earlier" in a girl's education. Many B.A. programs require, or strongly recommend, at least three semesters of high school algebra—rather than just one year—as well as trigonometry and geometry, the core trio of biology, chemistry, and physics, and AP biology classes where available.[7]

Environmental Science and Technology

Environmental science careers and majors in college typically require some experience in and aptitude with geography—an area where females tend to underenroll in comparison to males—as well as physics, biology, and chemistry.

The Timing and Sequencing of Math/Science Classes

Although Algebra I and geometry enrollment are crucial indicators of gender equity, equally important is the timing of these courses in a student's K–12 career. Do boys take Algebra I earlier in their education—in the seventh grade, for example—than girls? Are more boys on the mathematics fast track than girls? If so, future inequities may emerge not in the numbers of boys and girls who end high school having taken particular math classes, but in the numbers who take these classes early enough in their education to move quickly to advanced work in their high school and postsecondary careers.

What to Watch: For the 21st century, the critical gender equity problem may not be generic math and science preparation or the quantity of math taken, but also girls' timely enrollment in prerequisite courses for study in emerging fields such as computer science, biotechnology, and environmental science.

Technology

Advocates of technology-rich education speak optimistically about its potential to alleviate economic and racial inequities in resources and outcomes. But computer technology's tremendous growth in the public schools precedes any clear understanding of how best to integrate and use technology in the classroom to advance goals such as "constructivist," or hands-on, learning. Furthermore, as this report shows, preliminary evidence suggests that girls tend to have a more circumscribed, limited, and cautious interaction with technology than boys—both within and outside of schools. For technology to fulfill its promise as a leveler of educational inequalities, more research needs to be conducted on the ways that males and females, both students and K–12 educators, are using computer resources. Equity between the classes cannot be achieved through technology at the expense of equity between the sexes.

We need more research and debate, too, on the kinds of ideals, values, and perspectives on learning and knowledge that the "technoculture" promulgates. Education researcher Maxine Greene, among others, cautions that the "technical perspective" in reform efforts "assumes the school's main mission is to meet the national economic and technical needs." Others challenge that teachers have little sense of efficacy about technology, and tend to view it passively, following cues from policymakers, as the next "inevitability." Their "resistance" to technology, in turn, is seen as a pathology—the "technophobic" teacher—rather than a legitimate skepticism about technology's value and role in the learning process.[8]

What to Watch: Gender differences must become part of the equity discussion surrounding technology now, before computers become integral to teaching and schools. Do plans for integrating technology into the public schools take into account the needs and experiences of specific groups of students? Are all students envisioned as creative "power users," or are students informally tracked into different relationships with technology based on sex, class, or other social characteristics? How might technological products advance better—and more equitable—forms of learning and instruction generally?

College Admissions and Testing

The gender equity question surrounding high stakes tests historically has focused on the fairness of the test design itself. For example, does the SAT's multiple choice format or its selection of reading passages favor boys? However, high-stakes standardized tests, as described in this update, comprise just one part of a student's overall admissions portfolio.

Recent developments suggest that admissions practices may be changing to ensure campus diversity and educational opportunity. The University of California system may recommend, for example, automatic admission for the top four percent of students in each state high school, a policy that would magnify the importance of high school grades (where girls typically excel) and minimize the significance of SAT scores (where boys typically outscore girls).[9]

At the same time, AP course enrollment and exams appear to be growing in use and significance. Trends in AP enrollment and test-taking patterns are areas to watch in the future.

What to Watch: *It will be important to monitor test scores in the context of overall admissions processes and goals, and to assess changes in admissions policies for their potential impact on gender equity in access and enrollment. Future assessments of gender equity in high-stakes tests should monitor not only disparities in scores, but also how those scores are integrated into other components of a student's admissions portfolio, and how other features of the admissions process may affect groups of students differently.*

School Reform

Gender largely has been overlooked in the equity discussion surrounding charter schools, vouchers, home schooling, and other structural reforms in public education. Equity research has focused instead on the school reform's potential to minimize class disparities in outcome. If these reform trends continue to gain popularity, it will be crucial to assess what effects, if any, they are having on the gender equity agenda. Reforms deemed successful for *all* students in the abstract may not benefit specific groups of students within the schools to the same extent that they benefit other groups.

The possibility that some education reforms may benefit some groups of students more than others underscores the imperative that the high standards movement incorporate equity concerns.

Several reform movements, including charter and home schooling, for example, champion local and parental control over education, and decry "interventions" by the federal government. Their positions invite some questions: Does a standards-driven charter school, whose contract renewal hinges on its students' satisfactory test performance, facilitate or impede the remediation of gender gaps in performance? Do charter schools foster more or less equitable learning environments and pedagogical approaches? How does home schooling, currently practiced for one million students and growing at a 20 percent rate per year, affect the intellectual and social development of girls, especially given that many parents opt for home schooling to inculcate traditional, conservative ideologies and to shelter their children from the culture that they reject in the public schools?

From another perspective, some parents opt for home schooling arrangements because they fear that traditional gender stereotypes and harassment in the public schools will hinder their girls' intellectual growth. Equity issues, one researcher concludes, "will almost certainly remain a central focus of future research" on experimental schools and home schooling. This research focus on equity, however, should not be confined to class and race, but extended to consider gender as well.[10]

What to Watch: *At this point it is unclear what different effects, if any, broad changes in the structure and philosophy of public education may have on girls' and boys' opportunities and outcomes. Presumably, however, as the philosophy of public education changes, so, too, do the educational prospects and fortunes of specific groups of students that the schools serve. Because groups of students often require different things to achieve a good education, they may, by the same logic, be affected differently by changes in school type, organization, climate, and philosophy. As the Consortium for Policy Research in Education recommends, school reform evaluations must disaggregate their effects, since "a program may have persuasive evidence of effectiveness but this may mask its relative ineffectiveness with certain groups of students."*

The question, at least, invites further attention and consideration in the research and policy fields.[11]

To monitor these emerging educational issues, as well as the topic areas reviewed in this report, researchers need access to better, more specific data on educational outcomes and experiences. Currently, a lack of data on educational outcomes broken down by sex impedes efforts to establish baselines from which to monitor change and progress. Furthermore, lack of data disaggregated by race and gender tends to mask often significant "intra-gender" differences.

Our overarching—and crucial—recommendation, then, is that data must be made available on the educational experiences and outcomes of all students. As San Francisco school superintendent Waldemar Rojas has concluded, "If you don't disaggregate your data, you won't get at the problem." Current and planned data collection projects should disaggregate data by gender, race, ethnicity, and social class. The next section of this chapter provides a chart of potential baseline measures, drawn from this report, on selected indicators of gender equity.

Finally, a second overarching recomendation is that reforms to promote high educational standards for *all* students take into account what *specific* groups of students need to achieve high standards. As this report has demonstrated, equity and excellence are inherently linked. For future reforms to advance excellent education, they must work to advance equitable education.

SELECTED BASELINE MEASURES FOR GENDER EQUITY

◆

Subject	Baseline Measure
Course Taking	[Source: National Center for Educational Statistics, 1994]
Physics	22% of females and 27% of males had taken or were taking physics.
The Core Courses of Biology, Chemistry, and Physics	20% of females and 23% of males had taken or were taking the three core science courses.
Algebra I	68% of females and 65% of males had taken or were taking Algebra I.
Geometry	72% of females and 68% of males had taken or were taking geometry.
Computer Applications	2% of females and 6% of males had taken or were taking computer applications courses.
Computer Science	27% of females and 30% of males had taken or were taking computer science courses.
Spanish Language	48% of males and 55% of females had taken or were taking Spanish courses.
Music	45% of females and 27% males had taken or were taking music courses.

AP Course Taking

AP Physics   2% of females and 4% of males take AP Physics.

AP English   12% of males and 19% of females take AP English.

AP Foreign Languages 2% of males to 4% of females take AP foreign language courses.

AP Exam Taking

English   Females took 37 AP exams per 1,000 11th and 12th grade students; Males took 20 AP exams per 1,000.

Social Studies   Females took 36 AP exams per 1,000 11th and 12th grade students; Males took 29 AP exams per 1,000.

Foreign Language   Females took 11 AP exams per 1,000 11th and 12th grade students; Males took 6 AP exams per 1,000.

Calculus   Males took 18 AP exams per 1,000 11th and 12th grade students; Females took 16 AP exams per 1,000.

Science   Males took 19 AP exams per 1,000 11th and 12th grade students; Females took 17 exams per 1,000.

Computer Science   Males took 2 AP exams per 1,000 11th and 12th grade students; Females took no AP exams per 1,000.

SAT Scores   [Source: College Entrance Examination Board and Educational Testing Service, 1997]

Mean SAT Math Score   494 for females; 530 for males

Mean SAT Verbal Score 503 for females; 508 for males

Percentage of SAT Math Scores at 600 or Above   19% of females and 30% of males score at 600 or above.

Technology

[Source: NCES, NELS88 Follow-up Survey, 1992]

Use of Personal Computers

28% of males and 19% of females use a personal computer at least once a week.

Teacher Education

[Source: Sanders, National Survey on Teacher Education, 1993–94]

Time Spent on Gender Equity

68% of teacher education instructors spend two hours or less per semester on gender equity.

Grade Retention and Dropout Rates

[Source: Department of Education, Dropout Rates in the U.S., 1995]

Percentage of students age 16-24 retained

17% of males to 10% of females

Dropout Rates

Females comprised 45% of 15–24 year olds who dropped out in 1995; males, 55%.

Hispanic Dropout Rate

30% of Hispanic females age 16 to 24 are high school dropouts; 30% of Hispanic males are high school dropouts.

Retention and Dropout eventuInteraction

22% of males to 28% of females retained ally drop out.

<u>Teen Pregnancy</u>

Teen Pregnancy Rate

55% of all pregnant women were teenagers.

<u>Sports</u>

Sports Participation

33% of females to 50% of males took part in high school sports.

Other Extracurricular Activities

[Source: National Center for Education Statistics, 1992]

Student Government

13% of male 12th graders and 18% of female 12th graders participated.

Academic Honor Society

14% of male 12th graders and 23% of female 12th graders participated.

School Yearbook or Newspaper	14% of male 12th graders and 24% of female 12th graders participated.
School Service Clubs	10% of male 12th graders and 17% of female 12th graders participated.
School Academic Clubs	23% of male 12th graders and 27% of female 12th graders participated.

Cheryl L. Sattler is a research analyst at the Pelavin Research Center of the American Institutes for Research in Washington, DC. She is the author of *Talking About a Revolution: The Politics and Practice of Feminist Teaching* (Hampton Press, 1997) and *Teaching to Transform: Educating Women About Domestic Violence* (forthcoming from SUNY Press). Her research focuses on gender issues within K–12 and informal education, educational reform, and domestic violence. She is currently evaluating teacher professional development and correctional education. A former teacher, she earned her doctorate in educational foundations and policy studies from Florida State University.

Rita J. Kirshstein is managing associate at the Pelavin Research Center of the American Institutes for Research. Throughout her career she has studied gender equity and the needs of special populations. In 1997 she prepared the report *Women and Minority Faculty in Science and Engineering* (co-authored with Cheryl Sattler) for the National Science Foundation, and in 1995 she wrote *A Comprehensive Evaluation of Postsecondary Educational Opportunities for Persons Who Are Deaf and Hard of Hearing* for the U.S. Department of Education. Her current research and evaluation work focuses on educational technology, school reform, and higher education finance. She chaired the Commission for Women in Montgomery County (Maryland) in 1986-87 and developed several policy reports on family-oriented personnel policies and the needs of employed parent families. Formerly, as an assistant professor at the University of Virginia, she taught courses in women's studies and gender roles, as well as the sociology of education and higher education. She earned her doctorate in sociology from the University of Massachusetts/Amherst.

Elizabeth M. Rowe is a research analyst at the Pelavin Research Center of the American Institutes for Research. She is completing her doctoral studies in human development at Cornell University. Her dissertation, "The Transition to Algebra: The Crossroads in Math Self-Concept Development," focuses on gender issues in middle school mathematics education.

Erica L. deFur is a research assistant at the Pelavin Research Center of the American Institutes for Research. She received her bachelor of arts in psychology at the College of William & Mary, and conducted her senior research project on sexual harassment. She works on adult literacy and assessment issues for the National Center for Education Statistics. In addition she works on issues pertaining to children with emotional or behavioral problems for the Center for Effective Collaboration and Practice.

Kristin M. Kleimann is a research assistant at the Pelavin Research Center of the American Institutes for Research. She received her bachelor of arts in psychology and women's studies from Smith College, where she conducted an independent study on the development of a feminist identity. She is now helping to develop voluntary national tests in reading and mathematics. She is also assessing and evaluating School-to-Work institutes for state, local, and regional partnerships for implementing School-to-Work initiatives.

Pamela Haag is a senior research associate with the AAUW Educational Foundation. Previously, she was a postdoctoral fellow at the Pembroke Center for Research on Women, Brown University, and before that, a fellow at the Rutgers Center for Historical Analysis. She has received fellowships from the National Endowment for the Humanities and the Mellon Foundation. Her book *Historical Essays on Sexual Consent and American Liberalism* is scheduled for publication in spring 1999 from Cornell University Press. Haag received her doctorate from Yale University, where she specialized in American cultural history and gender studies.

Peer Reviewers

Cornelia Brunner, associate director and media designer, Center for Children and Technology, Educational Development Center, New York, NY
Christopher Cross, president, Council for Basic Education, Washington, DC.
Amanda Datnow, professor, University of California— Berkeley
Signithia Fordham, professor, University of Maryland— Baltimore County
Robert Orrill, executive director, Office of Academic Affairs, The College Board, Princeton, NJ
Paul Ramsey, vice president of School and College Services, Educational Testing Service, New York, NY
Ramsey Selden, director, Education Statistics Services Institute, Washington, DC
Charol Shakeshaft, professor, Hofstra University
Jonathan Supovitz, Consortium for Policy Research in Education, University of Pennsylvania
Barrie Thorne, professor, University of California—Berkeley
Olga Welch, professor, University of Tennessee, Knoxville

E N D N O T E S

Introduction

1. U.S. Department of Education, Office of Educational Research and Improvement, National Center for Education Statistics, *Digest of Educational Statistics 1997* (Washington, DC, 1997): 58.
2. Ibid., 60.
3. Lynn Schnaiberg, "U.S. Report Tracks High Dropout Rate Among Hispanics," *Education Week* 17, no. 22 (February 11, 1998): 7.
    Angela McGlynn, "Hispanic Women, Academia and Retention," *Hispanic Outlook* (February 13, 1998): 12.
4. Jeff Archer, "Surge in Hispanic Student Enrollment Predicted," *Education Week* 15, no. 27 (March 27, 1996): 3.
5. National School Safety Center, http://nssc1.org/latenews.htm, May 20, 1998.
6. Virginia B. Edwards et al., "The Urban Challenge," *Education Week* 17, no. 17 (January 8, 1998): 6.
7. Craig D. Jerald et al., "The State of the States," *Education Week* 17, no. 17 (January 8, 1998): 76–89.
    Goals 2000: Educate America Act of 1994, Public Law 103–227, 103rd Congress, 1st Session (31 March 1994)
    Title I National Education Goals
8. Andrew Trotter, "Taking Technology's Measure: Technology Counts Report," *Education Week* 17, no. 11 (November 10, 1997): 6–11.
9. Valerie E. Lee, "Is Single-Sex Secondary Schooling a Solution to the Problem of Gender Inequity," in *Separated by Sex: A Critical Look at Single-Sex Education for Girls*

(Washington, DC: American Association of University Women Educational Foundation, March 1998): 41.

10. Joan Scott, "Deconstructing Equality v. Difference, or the Uses of Poststructuralist Theory for Feminism," *Feminist Studies* 14 (Spring 1988): 33–50.

11. Ellen Wahl, *The Case for Equity and Excellence in Math and Science Education* (Washington, DC: Collaboration for Equity, The American Association for the Advancement of Science, 1997).

12. Maurice R. Berube, "The Politics of National Standards," *The Clearing House* 69, no. 3 (1996): 151–153.

    Ruth K. Blank et al., *Mathematics and Science Content Standards and Curriculum Frameworks: State Progress on Development and Implementation* (Washington, DC: Council of Chief State School Officers, 1997).

13. Bernice Resnick Sandler et al., *The Chilly Classroom: A Guide to Improve the Education of Women* (Washington, DC: National Association for Women in Education, 1996).

14. *Shortchanging Girls, Shortchanging America: A Call to Action*, (Washington, DC: American Association of University Women, 1991): 27.

    Carol Gilligan, *In a Different Voice: Psychological Theory and Women's Development* (Cambridge, MA: Harvard University Press, 1982).

15. David Tyack, *1990: Learning Together: A History of Coeducation in American Public Schools* (Hartford: Yale University Press, 1990): 2.

16. Jane B. Kahle, "Opportunities and Obstacles: Science Education in the Schools," in *The Equity Education: Fostering the Advancement of Women in the Sciences* (San Francisco: Jossey-Bass, 1996).

    Jo Sanders, "How Do We Get Educators to Teach Gender Equity?," in *Equity in the Classroom: Towards Effective Pedagogy for Girls and Boys*, eds. Patricia F. Murphy and Caroline V. Gipps (London: The Falmer Press, 1996): 214–227.

    Jo Sanders, "Teacher Education and Gender Equity," *ERIC Digest*, ED408277 (Washington, DC: ERIC Clearinghouse on Teaching and Teacher Education, May 1997).

    Wahl, *The Case for Equity.*

    Patricia B. Campbell and Karen Steinbrueck, *Striving for Gender Equity: National Programs to Increase Student Engagement with Math and Science* (Washington, DC: Collaboration for Equity, Fairness in Science and Mathematics Education, 1996).

    Cinda-Sue Davis et al., *The Equity Equation: Fostering the Advancement of Women in the Sciences, Mathematics, and Engineering* (San Francisco: Jossey-Bass, 1996).

    Sue V. Rosser, *Teaching the Majority: Breaking the Gender Barrier in Science, Mathematics, and Engineering* (New York: Teachers College Press, 1995).

    Sue V. Rosser, *Re-Engineering Female Friendly Science* (New York: Teachers College Press, 1997).

    Carole S. Hollenshead, "Exploring Explanations for Gender Differences in High

School Students' Science Achievement" (remarks at the annual meeting of the American Educational Research Association, Chicago, 24–28 March 1997).

Rolf Blank and Doreen Gruebel, *State Indicators of Science and Mathematics Education: State by State Trends and New Indicators from the 1993-1994 School Year* (Washington, DC: Council of Chief State School Officers, 1995).

U.S. Department of Education, Office of Educational Research and Improvement, National Center for Education Statistics, *Vocational Course Taking and Achievement: An Analysis of High School Transcripts and 1990 NAEP Assessment Scores* (Washington, DC, 1995).

Michael Kane and Sol Pelavin, *Changing the Odds: Factors Increasing Access to College* (New York: The College Board, 1990).

Sanders, "Teacher Education and Gender Equity."

Sue V. Rosser, *Female-Friendly Science* (Elmsford, NY: Pergamon Press, 1990).

Rosser, *Re-Engineering Female Friendly Science.*

James Collins, "How Johnny Should Read," *Time* 150, no. 17 (October 27, 1997).

Chapter One

1. Valerie Lee, "Is Single-Sex Secondary a Solution to the Problem of Gender Inequity?" in *Separated by Sex: A Critical Look at Single Sex-Education* (Washington, DC: American Association of Women Educational Foundation, March 1998): 42.

2. Rolf Blank and Doreen Gruebel, *State Indicators of Science and Mathematics Education: State by State Trends and New Indicators from the 1993-1994 School Year* (Washington, DC: Council of Chief State School Officers, 1995).

   U.S. Department of Education, Office of Educational Research and Improvement, National Center for Education Statistics, *Vocational Course Taking and Achievement: An Analysis of High School Transcripts and 1990 NAEP Assessment Scores* (Washington, DC, 1995).

3. Throughout this report, statistical significance is reported either when such tests were noted in the material reviewed for this report or when the appropriate information was provided allowing calculation of such tests. Several test procedures were used depending upon the nature of the data. Significance levels of .10, .05, and .01 are noted on the tables. A finding that is statistically significant at the .05 level, for example, means that there is less than 5 percent chance that the differences can be attributed to random variation.

4. Michael Kane and Sol Pelavin, *Changing the Odds: Factors Increasing Access College* (New York: The College Board, 1990).

5. Attention to and concern for the underrepresentation of women in mathematics and science fields has resulted in numerous gender equity initiatives focusing on these two curriculum areas (for example, the National Science Foundation's

Program for Women and Girls, the Women's Educational Equity Clearinghouse within the U.S. Department of Education; the Collaboration for Equity Among the American Association for the Advancement of Science; Girls, Inc; Educational Development Center, Inc.; and Campbell-Kibler Associates, Inc.

6. "Females Taking More Math Courses Than Males," http://www.act.org, April 23, 1998.

7. Ruth K. Blank et al., *Mathematics and Science Content Standards and Curriculum Frameworks: State Progress on Development and Implementation* (Washington, DC: Council of Chief State School Officers, 1997).

8. Campbell and Steinbrueck, *Striving for Gender Equity*.
   Davis et al. *The Equity Equation*.
   Rosser, *Re-Engineering Female Friendly Science*.

9. Sue V. Rosser, *Female-Friendly Science* (Elmsford, NY: Pergamon Press, 1990).
   Sue. V. Rosser, *Re-Engineering Female Friendly Science* (New York: Teachers College Press, 1997).

10. James Collins, "How Johnny Should Read," *Time* 150, no. 17 (October 27, 1997).

11. Arthur Halbrook and Katherine Woodward, *National and State Content Standards in English Language Arts* (Washington, DC: GED Testing Service, American Council on Education): 3.

12. With the exception of English composition in 1990, these differences are not statistically significant. We report these findings, however, because of the consistent direction of the differences and the importance of discussing and monitoring boys' participation in the English/language arts curriculum.

13. Nancy Cole and Warren W. Willingham, *Gender and Fair Assessment*, (Princeton: Educational Testing Service, Mahwah, NJ: Lawrence Erlbaum Associates, 1997): 122.

14. Elizabeth Hayes and Jennifer Hopkins, "Gender Literacy Learning: Implications for Research in Adult Literacy Education" (paper presented at the annual meeting of the American Educational Research Association (New York: April 1995): 15.

15. Elaine Millard, "Differently Literate: Gender Identity and the Construction of the Developing Reader," *Gender and Education* 9, no. 1 (March 1997): 31–48.

16. Kathleen Gormley et al., "Gender Differences in Classroom Writing: An Analysis of Sixth Grade Students' Reader Response Entries," *ERIC Digests ED353578* (Washington, DC: ERIC Clearinghouse, 1992).

17. Rebecca Cummings, "11th Graders View Gender Differences in Reading and Math," *Journal of Reading* 38, no. 3 (November 1994): 196–99.

18. Eileen McKenna, "Gender Differences in Reading Attitudes" (master's thesis, Kean College of New Jersey: May 1997).

19. *Women, Minorities, and Persons with Disabilities in Science and Engineering: 1996* (Washington, DC: National Science Foundation, 1996).

20. Elaine Woo, "Classroom Renaissance," *LA Times*, 4 February 1997.

21. Although not statistically significant, we note these findings because we believe the apparent widening gap between males and females deserves monitoring.

22. Linda K. Bunker et al., *The President's Council on Physical Fitness and Sports Report: Physical Activity and Sports in the Lives of Girls* (Washington, DC: President's Council on Physical Fitness and Sports, 1997).

23. U.S. Department of Education, Office of Educational Research and Improvement, National Center for Education Statistics, *Digest of Educational Statistics 1997* (Washington, DC, 1997).

24. Jeannie Oakes, "Can Tracking Inform Practice? Technical, Normative, and Political Considerations," *Educational Researcher* 21, no. 4 (1992a): 12–21.
    Jeannie Oakes, "Detracking Schools: Early Lessons from the Field," *Phi Delta Kappan* 73, no. 4 (1992b): 448–54.
    Relsa N. Page, *Lower Track Classrooms: A Curricular Perspective* (New York: Teachers College Press, 1991).

25. Maureen T. Hallinan, "School Differences in Tracking Effects on Achievement," *Social Forces* 72, no. 3 (March 1994): 799–820.

26. Jomills Henry Braddock II and Robert E. Slavin, "Why Ability Grouping Must End: Achieving Excellence and Equity in American Education," *Beyond Tracking: Finding Success in Inclusive Schools*, eds., H. Pool and J. A. Page (Bloomington: Phi Delta Kappa Educational Foundation, 1995): 7–20.

27. M. L. Wehmeyer and M. Schwartz, "Disproportionate Representation of Males in Special Education Services: Biology, Behavior or Bias" (Gender Equity in Special Education, unpublished).
    M. Wagner, "Being Female—A Secondary Disability? Gender Differences in the Transition Experiences of Young People with Disabilities" (prepared for presentation to the Special Education Special Interest Group of the American Education Research Association annual meeting, San Francisco, 1992).
    Wagner et al., "Youth with Disabilities: How Are They Doing? The First Comprehensive Report From the National Longitudinal Transition Study of Special Education Students" (prepared for the Office of Special Education Programs and the U.S. Department of Education, SRI International, 1991).
    D. L. Caseau et al., "Special Education Services for Girls with Serious Emotional Disturbance: A Case of Gender Bias?," *Behavorial Disorders* 20, no.1 (1994): 51–60.

28. Sally M. Reis and Carolyn M. Callahan, "My Boyfriend, My Girlfriend, or Me: The Dilemma of Talented Teenaged Girls," *The Journal of Secondary Gifted Education* 7, no. 4 (1996): 434–446.

29. Nancy Kreinberg and Ellen Wahl, eds. *Thoughts and Deeds: Equity in Mathematics and Science Education* (Washington, DC.: American Association for the Advancement of Science, Collaboration for Equity, 1997).
    Jane B. Kahle, "Opportunities and Obstacles: Science Education in the Schools," in Cinda-Sue Davis et al., *The Equity Equation: Fostering the Advancement of Women in*

the Sciences, Mathematics, and Engineering (San Francisco: Jossey-Bass, 1996): 57–95.

30. Peter M. Hall, ed. *Race, Ethnicity, and Multiculturalism: Policy and Practice*, Missouri Symposium on Research in Educational Policy, vol. 1 (New York: Garland Publishing, 1997).

Barbara J. Bank and Peter M. Hall, eds., *Gender, Equity and Schooling: Policy and Practice*, Missouri Symposium on Symposium on Research and Educational Policy, vol. 2 (New York: Garland Publishing Inc., 1997).

31. Susan L. Dauber et al, "Tracking and Transition through the Middle Grades: Channeling Educational Trajectories," *Sociology of Education* 69, no. 4 (October 1996): 290–307.

32. Gail Crombie et al, "Gifted Programs: Gender Differences in Referral and Enrollment," *Gifted Child Quarterly* 36, no. 4 (1992): 212–213.

Carolyn Reeves, "Read, Achievement and Career Choices: Comparisons of Males and Females, Gender Distribution in Program for the Gifted," *Roeper Review* 13, no. 4 (1991).

Digest of Education Statistics 1997.

33. Pat O'Connell Ross, *National Excellence: A Case for Developing America's Talent* (Washington, DC: U.S. Department of Education, Office of Educational Research and Improvement, National Center for Educational Statistics, October 1993).

Thomas J. Ward et al., "Examination of a New Protocol for the Identification of At-Risk Gifted Learners" (paper presented at the annual meeting of the American Educational Research Association, San Francisco, April 1992).

34. Ross, *National Excellence.*

35. Carolyn Reeves Read, "Achievement and Career Choices: Comparisons of Males and Females, Gender Distribution in Program for the Gifted," *Roper Review* 13, no. 4 (1991)

36. Ibid.

37. Sally M. Reis and M. Katherine Gavin, *Why Jane Doesn't Think She Can Do Math: How Teachers Can Encourage Talented Girls in Mathematics* (Reston, VA: National Council of Teachers of Mathematics, in press).

38. Donna Siegel and Sally M. Reis, "Gender Differences in Teacher and Student Perceptions of Student Ability and Effort," *The Journal of Secondary Gifted Education* (Winter 1994/1995): 86–92.

39. Ross, *National Excellence.*

40. Signithia Fordham, "Those Loud Black Girls: (Black) Women, Silence, and Gender Passing in the Academy," *Anthropology and Education Quarterly* 24, no. 1 (1993): 3–32.

Signithia Fordham, *Blacked Out: Dilemmas of Race, Identity, and Success at Capital High* (Chicago: The University of Chicago Press, 1996).

41. Fordham, "Those Loud Black Girls."

....

42. Research for Action, Inc., Jody Cohen and Sukey Blanc et al., *Girls in the Middle: Working to Succeed in School* (Washington, DC: American Association of University Women Educational Foundation, 1996).

43. Virginia B. Edwards et al., "The Urban Challenge," *Education Week* 17, no. 17 (January 8, 1998): 6.

44. Cole and Willingham, *Gender and Fair Assesment.*

Chapter Two

1. Carole S. Hollenshead, "Exploring Explanations for Gender Differences in High School Students' Science Achievement" (remarks at the annual meeting of the American Educational Research Association, Chicago, March 24–28, 1997).

2. Jonathan A. Supovitz, "From Multiple Choices to Multiple Choices, A Diverse Society Deserves a More Diverse Assesment System," *Education Week* 17 no. 10 (November 5, 1997): 34, 37.

3. Marcia Linn and Cathy Kessel, "Grades or Scores: Predicting Future College Mathematics Performance," *Educational Measurement: Issues and Practice* 15, no. 4 (Winter 1996): 10–14, 38.

4. U.S. Department of Education, Office of Educational Research and Improvement, National Center for Education Statistics, *The 1994 High School Transcript Study Tabulations* (Washington, DC, 1994).

   U.S. Department of Education, Office of Educational Research and Improvement, National Center for Education Statistics, *The 1994 High School Transcript Study Tabulations: Comparative Data on Credits Earned and Demographics for 1994, 1990, 1987, and 1982 High School Graduates* (Washington, DC, 1997).

   The High School Profile Report (Iowa City, IA: American College Testing Program, 1990–1997).

   College-Bound Seniors: A Profile of SAT Program Test Takers (New York: College Entrance Examination Board and Educational Testing Service 1997).

   Doris R. Entwisle et al., *Children, Schools, and Inequality,* Social Inequality Series (Boulder, CO: Westview Press, 1997).

5. U.S. Department of Education, Office of Educational Research and Improvement, National Center for Education Statistics, *NAEP 1996 Summary Data Tables* (Washington, DC, 1997).

   TIMSS International Study Center, *Highlights of the Results from TIMSS* (Boston College, November 1996).

   TIMSS International Study Center, *TIMSS Highlights from the Primary Grades* (Boston College, June 1997).

   TIMSS International Study Center, *TIMSS Highlights* (Boston College, February 1998).

6. TIMSS and NAEP differ in their design: TIMSS was designed around common curriculum from different countries, whereas NAEP is not tied to specific classroom content.

7. Albert E. Beaton et al., *Science Achievement in the Middle School Years: IEA's Third International Mathematics and Science Study (TIMSS)* (Chestnut Hill, MA: Center for the Study of Testing, Evaluation, and Educational Policy, Boston College, 1997).

8. U.S. Department of Education, Office of Educational Research and Improvement, National Center for Education Statistics, *NAEP 1996 Summary Data Tables* (Washington, DC, 1997).

9. Karen Chenowith, "A Measurement of What?" *Black Issues in Higher Education* 14, no. 14 (1997) 14: 18–22.

   George L. Garriques, "National Merit Scholarships: A Major Dash of Jim Crow," *Journal of Blacks in Higher Education* 3 (Spring 1994), pp. 60–64.

   Cecilia McCall, "Gender and Reading Assessment," *ERIC Digest* 320116, 1989.

10. Theresa Anne Cleary, Gender Differences in Aptitude and Achievement Test Scores," in *Sex Equity in Educational Opportunity, Achievement, and Testing: Proceedings of the 1991 ETS Invitational Conference* (Princeton, NJ, Educational Testing Service): 51–90.

    Nancy Cole and Warren W. Willingham, *Gender and Fair Assessment*, (Princeton: Educational Testing Service, Mahwah, NJ: Lawrence Erlbaum Associates, 1997): 76.

11. Cleary, "Gender Differences."

    Cole and Willingham, *Gender and Fair Assessment*, 122.

12. Ibid., 111.

13. *The High School Profile Report.*

14. *College-Bound Seniors: A Profile of SAT Program Test Takers.*

15. *The High School Profile Report.*

16. Kathleen Kennedy Manzo, "For Girls, Writing's on the Wall in New PSAT Exam," *Education Week* 17, no. 20 (January 28, 1998).

17. Halpern, "The Disappereance of Cognitive Gender Differences: What You See Depends on Where You Look," *American Psychology* 44, no. 8 (1989): 1156–1158.

    Jonathan A. Supovitz, "Mirror, Mirror on the Wall: Which is the Fairest Test of All? An Examination of the Equitability of Portfolio Assessment Relative to Standardized Tests," *Harvard Educational Review* 67, no. 3 (Fall 1997).

    Stephen P. Klein et al., "Gender and Racial/Ethnic Differences on Performance Assessments in Science," *Educational Evaluation and Policy Analysis* 19, no. 2 (Summer 1997): 83.

18. Supovitz, "From Multiple Choice to Multiple Choices."

Chapter Three

1. Patricia B. Campbell and Ellen Wahl, "What's Sex Got to Do With It? Simplistic Questions, Complex Answers," in *Separated by Sex: A Critical Look at Single-Sex Education for Girls* (Washington, DC: American Association of University Women Educational Foundation, March 1998): 70.

2. Milbrey W. McLaughlin and Lorrie A. Shepard, *Improving Education Through Standards-Based Reform* (Washington, DC: National Academy of Education Panel on Standards-Based Education Reform, 1995).

3. *Assessment Standards for School Mathematics* (Reston, VA: National Council for Teachers of Mathematics, 1995).

4. Jane B. Kahle, "Opportunities and Obstacles: Science Education in the Schools," in *The Equity Equation: Fostering the Advancement of Women in the Sciences, Mathematics, and Engineering*, eds., Cinda-Sue Davis et al. (San Francisco: Jossey-Bass, 1996): 57–95.

5. Daniel C. Humphrey and Patrick M. Shields, *A Review of the Mathematics and Science Curriculum Frameworks* (Menlo Park, CA: SRI International, April 1996).

6. Albert Shanker, *Making Standards Matter: A Fifty-State Progress Report on Efforts to Raise Academic Standards* (Washington, DC: American Federation of Teachers, Educational Issues Department, 1995).

   Rolf K. Blank et al., *Mathematics and Science Content Standards and Curriculum Frameworks: State Progress on Development and Implementation* (Washington, DC: Council of Chief State School Officers, 1997).

7. Humphrey and Shields, *A Review of the Mathematics and Science.*

8. McLaughlin and Shepard, *Improving Education.*

9. Susan M. Bailey and Patricia B. Campbell, "Gender Equity: The Unexamined Basic of School Reform," *Stanford Law and Policy Review* (1992): 73–86.

   Sue V. Rosser, *Re-Engineering Female Friendly Science* (New York: Teachers College Press, 1997).

10. Sue V. Rosser, *Female-Friendly Science* (Elmsford, NY: Pergamon Press, 1990).

    Sue V. Rosser, "Female Friendly Science: Including Women in Curricular Content and Pedagogy in Science," *The Journal of General Education* 42, no. 3 (1993): 191–220.

    Sue V. Rosser, *Teaching the Majority: Breaking the Gender Barrier in Science, Mathematics, and Engineering* (New York: Teachers College Press, 1995).

    Beatriz Chu Clewell et al., *Systemic Reform in Mathematics and Science Education: An Urban Perspective* (Washington, DC: The Urban Institute, 1995).

11. Rosser, *Re-Engineering Female Friendly Science.*

12. Valerie Lee, "Gender Equity and the Organization of Schools," in *Gender Equity, and Schooling.* New York: Garland Publishing, Inc. 1997). Barbara J. Bank and Peter M. Hall, *Gender, Equity and Schooling* (Washington, DC: Garland Publishing, Inc., 1997).

13. Sunny Hansen et al., *Growing Smart: What's Working for Girls in School* (Washington, DC: American Association of University Women Educational Foundation, 1995): 26, 29.

14. Jane B. Kahle and Judith Meece, "Research on Gender Issues in the Classroom," chapter 18 in *Handbook of Research in Science Teaching and Learning*, ed., Dorothy L. Gabel (New York: Macmillan, 1994).

15. Joe Sanders, "How Do We Get Educatoirs to Teach Gender Equity?," in *Equity in the Classroom: Towards Effective Pedagogy for Girls and Boys*, eds. Patricia F. Murphy and Caroline V. Gipps (London: The Falmer Press, 1996): 214–227.

16. Peggy Orenstein, in association with American Association for University Women, *School Girls: Young Women, Self-Esteem and the Confidence Gap* (New York: Doubleday, 1994).

17. Ibid.
    Myra and David Sadker, *Failing at Fairness: How Our Schools Cheat Girls* (New York: A Touchstone Book, 1995).

18. Bernice Resnick Sandler et al., *The Chilly Classroom Climate: A Guide to Improve the Education of Women* (Washington, DC: National Association for Women in Education, 1996): 9.
    Sandler and Hall have examined gender bias in higher education for more than two decades. Their work also has relevance for K–12 education.
    Sherrill Evenson Pryor, "Preservice Teacher Attitudes and Knowledge of Gender-Equitable Teaching Methods," in *Gender and Race on the Campus and in the School: Beyond Affirmative Action* (Washington, DC: American Association of University Women, 1997).

19. Clara C. Park, "Learning Style Preferences of Asian American (Chinese, Filipino, Korean, and Vietnamese) Students in Secondary Schools," *Equity & Excellence in Education* 30, no. 2 (1997): 68–77 .

20. Carole B. Shmurak and Thomas M. Ratliff, "Gender Equity and Gender Bias in the Classroom," *Research in Middle Level Education* 17, no. 2: 47–66.
    Carole B. Schmurak and Thomas M. Ratliff, "Gender Equity and Gender Bias: Issues for the Middle School Teacher," *Middle School Journal* 25, no. 5 (1994): 63–66.

21. Mary E. Yepez, "An Observation of Gender-Specific Behavior in the ESL Classroom," *A Journal of Research* 30, no. 1–2 (1994): 121–33.

22. Melody D'Ambrosio and Patricia S. Hammer, "Gender Equity in the Catholic Elementary Schools" (paper presented at the annual convention and exposition of the National Catholic Education Association, Philadelphia, April 1996).

23. Ibid.
    Myra Sadker and David Sadker, *Failing at Fairness: How Our Schools Cheat Girls* (New York: A Touchstone Book, 1995).

24. Mary K. Bendixen-Noe and Lynne Degler Hall, "The Quest for Gender Equity in America's Schools: From Preschool and Beyond," *Journal of Early Childhood Teacher Education* 17, no. 2 (1996): 50–57.
    Sandra Zaher, "Gender and Curriculum in the School Room," *Education Canada* 34, no. 1 (1996): 26–29.
    Carol Shakeshaft, "Reforming Science Education to Include Girls," *Theory into Practice* 34, no. 1 (1995): 74–79.
25. Valerie E. Lee, "Gender Equity and the Organization of Schools," in *Gender, Equity and Schooling* (New York: Garland Publishing, Inc., 1997).
26. Valerie E. Lee et al., "Sexism in Single-Sex and Coeducational Independent Secondary School Classrooms," *Sociology of Education* 67, no. 2 (1994): 92–120.
27. Ibid., 108.
28. Ibid., 109.
29. Irene Beck, "Gender Equity in Schools: Beyond Sugar and Spice," *PTA Today* 20 (Jan.-Feb. 1995): 11–13.
30. Dianne D. Horgan, *Achieving Gender Equity: Strategies for the Classroom* (Boston: Allyn & Bacon, 1995).
31. Ibid.
32. Horgan, *Achieving Gender Equity.*
33. Bernice Resnick Sandler et al., *The Chilly Classroom Climate: A Guide to Improve the Education of Women* (Washington, DC: National Association for Women in Education, 1996): 9.
34. Michelle Fine, *Framing Dropouts: Notes on the Politics of an Urban High School* (Albany, NY: SUNY, 1990).
35. Sadker and Sadker, *Failing at Fairness.*
36. Schmurak and Ratcliff, "Gender Equity and Gender Bias: Issues for the Middle School Teacher."
    Schmurak and Ratcliff, "Gender Equity and Gender Bias in the Classroom."
37. Jill McLean Taylor et al., *Between Voice and Silence: Women and Girls, Race and Relationship* (Cambridge: Harvard University Press, 1995).
38. Carla O'Connor, review of *Between Voice and Silence: Women and Girls, Race and Relationship,* by Jill McLean Taylor et al., *Contemporary Sociology: A Journal of Reviews* 26, no. 4 (1997): 507–508.
39. Michelle Fine et al., "Communities of Difference: A Critical Look at Desegregated Spaces Created for and by Youth," *Harvard Educational Review* 67, no. 2 (1997): 274–284.
40. Michele Foster, "African American Teachers and Culturally Relevant Pedagogy," chapter 31 in *Academic Achievements: Approaches, Theories and Research,* eds. James Banks and Cherry Banks (New York: Macmillan, 1995): 570–581.
41. Frances A. Maher, "Progressive Education and Feminist Pedagogy: Issues in Gender,

Power, and Authority," in *Gender and Race on the Campus and in the School: Beyond Affirmative Action*, (Washington, DC: American Association of University Women, 1997).

42. Beatriz Chu Clewell et al., *Breaking the Barriers. Helping Female and University Students Succeed in Science* (San Francisco: Jossey-Bass, 1992).

   Cinda-Sue Davis and Sue V. Rosser, "Program and Curricular Interventions," in *The Equity Equation*, eds. Cinda-Sue Davis et al. (San Francisco: Jossey-Bass, 1996): 232–264.

   Deborah A. Carey et al., "Equity and Mathematics Education," in *New Directions for Equity in Mathematics Education*, eds. Walter G. Secada, et al. (Cambridge: Harvard University Press, 1995): 93–125.

   Sandra L. Hanson, *Lost Talent: Women in the Sciences* (Philadelphia: Temple University Press, 1996).

   Lesley H. Parker et al., *Gender, Science, and Mathematics Shortening the Shadow* (Science and Technology Education Library, Boston: Kluwer Academic Publishers, 1996).

   Rosser, "Female-Friendly Science: Including Women in Curricular Content and Pedagogy in Science," 191–220.

   Rosser, *Teaching the Majority.*

   Rosser, *Re-Engineering Female Friendly Science.*

   Jo Sanders, *Lifting the Barriers: 600 Strategies that Really Work to Increase Girls' Participation in Science, Mathematics, and Computers* (New York: Jo Sanders Publications, 1994).

   Jo Sanders, "How Do We Get Educators to Teach Gender Equity?" in *Equity in the Classroom: Towards Effective Pedagogy for Girls and Boys*, eds. Patricia F. Murphy and Caroline V. Gipps (London: The Falmer Press, 1995): 214–227.

   Walter G. Secada et al., eds. *New Directions for Equity in Mathematics Education* (Cambridge: Harvard University Press, 1995).

   Jo Sanders, "Women in Technology: Attribution, Learned Helplessness, Self-Esteem, and Achievement (presented at the Conference on Women, Girls, and Technology, Tarytown, NY, Marymount Institute for the Education of Women and Girls, November 1997).

43. Fred M. Newmann et al., "Student Engagement and Achievement in American Secondary Schools," in chapter 1, *The Significance and Sources of Student Engagement*, ed., Fred M. Newmann (New York: Teachers College Press, 1992): 23.

44. *How Schools Shortchange Girls: The AAUW Report, A Study of Major Findings on Girls and Education* (Washington, DC: American Association of University Women Educational Foundation, New York: Marlowe and Company 1995): 116.

45. Jay R. Campbell et al., *NAEP 1996 Trends in Academic Progress* (Washington, DC: U. S. Department of Education, National Office of Educational Research and Improvement, Center for Education Statistics, 1997).

Rosser, *Re-Engineering Female Friendly Science*.

National Research Council, *National Science Education Standards* (Washington, DC: National Academy Press, 1996).

46. Nancy Kreinberg, "Equity and Systemic Reform," in *Collaboration for Equity* (Washington, DC: American Association for the Advancement of Science, 1996).

   Campbell et al., *NAEP 1996 Trends in Academic Progress*.

   Jane B. Kahle and A. Damnjanovic, "The Effect of Inquiry Activities on Elementary Students Enjoyment, Ease, and Confidence in Doing Science: An Analysis by Sex and Race," *Journal of Women and Minorities in Science and Engineering* 1 (1994): 17–28.

   Jane B. Kahle, "What We Have Learned: A Reformed Researcher's Perspective" (paper prepared for the National Science Foundation, Grant #OSR-92500, n.d.).

   S. M. Malcolm, "Science for All: Easy to Say, Hard to Do," in *In Pursuit of Excellence: National Standards for Science Education*, ed. A. Pendergast (proceedings of the AAAS Forum for School Science, Washington, DC, 1992).

47. David T. Burkham et al., "Gender and Science Learning Early in High School: Subject Matter and Laboratory Experiences," *American Educational Research Journal* 34, no. 2 (1997): 297–331.

48. F. Hughes-McDonnell, *Understanding High School Physics Students Perspectives of Their Classroom Experiences and Their Images of Physics and Physicists: A Pilot Study* (Cambridge: Harvard Graduate School of Education, 1996).

49. Ibid., 67.

50. Gloria E. Napper-Owen, "And Justice for All: Equity in the Elementary Classroom," *Strategies* 8, no. 3 (1994): 23–26.

   Jepkorir Rose Chepyator-Thomson and Catherine D. Ennis, "Reproduction and Resistance to the Culture of Femininity and Masculinity in Secondary School Physical Education," *Research Quarterly for Exercise and Sport* 68 (March 1997): 89–99.

51. Sharon Nelson-Barber and Elise Trumbull Estrin, "Bringing Native American Perspectives to Mathematics and Science Teaching," *Theory into Practice* 34, no. 3 (Summer 1995): 174–185.

52. Fine et al., "Communities of Difference," 274–284.

53. Foster, "African American Teachers."

54. Nitza M. Hidalgo et al., "Research on Families, Schools, Communities: A Multicultural Perspective," in *Academic Achievement: Approaches, Theories, and Research* (1995): 502.

55. Lyn Reese, "Gender Equity and Texts," *Social Studies Review* 33 (Winter 1994): 12–15.

56. Kathleen Kennedy Manzo, "Glimmer of History Standards Show Up in Latest Textbooks," *Education Week* 17, no. 6 (October 8, 1997): 1, 11.

57. Shmurak and Ratliff, "Gender Equity and Gender Bias: Issues for the Middle School Teacher."

Shmurak and Ratliff, "Gender Equity and Gender Bias in the Classroom."

58. Christine E. Beyer, "Gender Representation in Illustrations, Text and Topic Areas in Sexuality Education Curricula," *Journal of School Health* 66 (December 1996): 361–64.

59. Manzo, "Glimmer of History Standards."

    Anne Chapman, *A Great Balancing Act: Equitable Education for Girls and Boys* (Washington, DC: National Association of Independent Schools, 1997).

60. Research for Action, Inc., *Girls in the Middle*, 74.

61. Gloria Ladson-Billings, "Multicultural Teacher Education: Research, Practice, and Policy," in James Banks and Cherry Banks, eds., *The Handbook of Research on Multicultural Education* (New York: Macmillan, 1995): 747–759.

62. Julian Guthrie, "Book List Approval a Story of Passion, Negotiation," *San Francisco Examiner*, 23 March 1998, p. 1.

63. U.S. Department of Education, Office of Educational Research and Improvement, National Center for Education Statistics, *Digest of Education Statistics 1996* (Washington, DC, 1996): Table 227.

64. "Texas May Drop All Textbooks, for Laptops," *New York Times*, November 19, 1997.

65. *Computers and Classrooms: The Status of Technology in U.S. Schools* (Princeton, NJ: Educational Testing Service, 1997).

66. "Texas May Drop All Textbooks, for Laptops."

67. Hanson, *Lost Talent: Women in the Sciences*, 1.

68. Teresa Greenfield, "Girls and Boys Use of Interactive Science Museums (paper presented at the American Education Research Association meeting, San Francisco, 1995).

    Sanders, "Women in Technology."

69. Janese Swanson, "A Conversation with Janese Swanson," (speech at the Conference on Women, Girls, and Technology, Tarrytown, NY, The Marymount Institute for the Education of Women and Girls, November 11, 1997).

70. Margaret Honey, *For the Maternal Voice in the Technological Universe* (paper presented at the Girls and Technology conference, Marymount University, Tarrytown, NY, 1997).

71. Montgomery County, MD, Department of Educational Accountability, in a fax to American Institutes for Research, 1998, Montgomery County, MD Public Schools.

72. Bernard E. Whitley, Jr., "Gender Differences in Computer-Related Attitudes and Behavior: A Meta-Analysis," *Computers in Human Behavior* 13, no. 1 (1997): 1–2.

73. Carole S. Nelson and J. Allen Watson, "The Computer Gender Gap: Children's Attitudes, Performance and Socialization. Spotlight: Gender Differences," *Montessori Life* 7 (Fall 1995): 33–35.

    Melissa Mangione, "Understanding the Critics of Educational Technology: Gender Inequalities and Computers 1983-1993" (in proceedings of the 1995 annual national convention of the Association for Educational Communications and Technology (AECT) Anaheim, CA, 1995).

L. J. Gurak and N. L. Bayer, "Making Gender Visible: Extending Feminist Critiques of Technology to Technical Communication," *Technical Communication Quarterly* 3 (Summer 1994): 257–70.

Melissa Koch, "Opening up Technology to Both Genders," *Technos* 3 (1994): 14–19.

74. Carol L. Hodes, "Gender Representations in Mathematics Software," *Journal of Educational Technology Systems* 24, no. 1 (1995–96): 67–73.

75. Staci Durham and Sheila Brownlow, "Sex Differences in the Use of Science and Technology in Children's Cartoons," *Journal of Science Education and Technology* 6, no. 2 (June 1997): 103–110.

76. Janice E. Woodrow et al., "The Impact of Technology Enhanced Science Instruction on Pedagogical Beliefs and Practices," *Journal of Science Education and Technology* 5, no. 3 (1994): 241–252.

77. Sanders, "Women in Technology."

Jeannie Margolis and Alan Fisher, "Women in Computer Sciences: Closing the Gender Gap in Higher Education" (second annual report to the Sloan Foundation, Carnegie Mellon University School of Computer Science, Pittsburgh, 1997).

78. Cornelia Brunner, associate director, Educational Development Center in a personal letter to Pamela Haag, research associate, 7 January 1998, American Association of University Women Educational Foundation, Washington, DC.

79. Ibid.

80. Jay Moskowitz et al., *Meeting the Challenges of a Teachers First Year: Lessons from around the Pacific Rim* (Washington, DC: Pelavin Research Institute, 1997).

Elizabeth Grinder and Pam Gordon, "Current Teacher Induction Practices in the United States" (background paper, Pelavin Research Institute, 1995).

Ronald N. Marso and Fred L. Pigge, "Teacher Mentor Induction Programs: An Assessment of First-Year Teachers" (paper presented at the annual meeting of the Association of Teacher Educators 70th Annual Conference, Las Vegas, Nevada, 1990).

F. McDonald, "The Problems of Beginning Teachers: A Crisis in Training," in volume 1 of a series, *A Study of Induction Programs for Beginning Teachers*, (Princeton, NJ: Educational Testing Service, 1980).

What Matters Most: Teaching for America's Future (New York: National Commission on Teaching and America's Future, 1996).

81. Patricia B. Campbell and Jo Sanders, "Uninformed But Interested: Findings of a National Survey on Gender Equity in Preservice Teacher Education," *Journal of Teacher Education* 48, no. 1 (1997): 69–75.

82. Ibid.

83. Jordan J. Titus, "Gender Messages in Education Foundations Textbooks," *Journal of Teacher Education* 44, no. 1 (1993): 38–44.

84. Sherrill Evenson Pryor, "Preservice Teacher Attitudes and Knowledge of Gender Equitable Teaching Methods," in *Gender and Race on the Campus and in the School: Beyond Affirmative Action* (Washington, DC: American Association of University Women, 1997): 275–285.

85. Jacqueline Jones and Edward Chittenden, "An Observational Study of NBPTS Candidates As They Progress Through the Certification Process" (symposium at the annual meeting of the American Educational Research Association, Chicago, 1997).

86. Karla Haworth, "Teacher-Education Accreditor Issues: Draft Standards for Training Programs," *The Chronicle of Higher Education* (October 1997).

87. *Draft Standards for Identifying and Supporting Quality Professional Development Schools* (Washington, DC: National Council for Accreditation of Teacher Education, 1997).

88. Sanders, "Women in Technology."

89. U.S. Department of Education, Office of Educational Research and Improvement, National Center for Education Statistics, *Projections of Education Statistics to 2000* (Washington, DC, 1997).

90. Jo Sanders, "How Do We Get Educators to Teacher Gender Equity?" in Patricia F. Murphy and Caroline V. Gipps, eds., *Equity in the Classroom: Towards Effective Pedagogy for Girls and Boys* (London: Falmer, 1995): 214–227.
Jo Sanders, Patricia Campbell, and Karin Steinbrueck, "One Project, Many Strategies: Making Preservice Teacher Education More Equitable," *Journal of Women and Minorities in Science and Engineering*, vol. 3 (1997): 225–243.

91. Ibid.

92. Titus, "Voices of Resistance."

93. Susan M. Bailey, "The Current Status of Gender Equity Research in American Schools," *Educational Psychologist* 24, no. 4 (1993): 321–339.

94. Campbell and Sanders, "Uninformed But Interested."

Chapter Four

1. Michelle Fine, *Framing Dropouts: Notes on the Politics of an Urban High School* (Albany, NY: SUNY, 1990).

2. Ray del Portillo and Margot M. Segura, foreword to *Cada cabeza es un mundo/Each Mind Is a World*, by Jose Antonio Burciaga et al. (Sausalito, California: The California Latino-Chicano High School Dropout Prevention Project, 1996).

3. *How Schools Shortchange Girls—The AAUW Report: A Study of Major Findings on Girls and Education* (Washington, DC: American Association of University Women Educational Foundation, New York: Marlowe and Company, 1995): 59.

4. Doris R. Entwisle et al., *Children, Schools, and Inequality*, Social Inequality Series (Boulder, CO: Westview Press, 1997).
   Elizabeth Rowe and John Eckenrode, "The Timing of Academic Difficulties Among Maltreated and Normal Treated Children" (paper presented at the biennial meeting of the Society for Research in Child Development, Indianapolis, IN, 1995).
   U.S. Department of Education, Office of Educational Research and Improvement, National Center for Education Statistics, *Dropout Rates in the United States: 1995* (Washington, DC, 1997).
5. Ibid.
6. Ibid.
7. Charol Shakeshaft, professor, Hofstra University, New York, in a personal letter to Pamela Haag, research associate, 5 February 1998, American Association of University Women Educational Foundation, Washington, DC.
8. *Dropout Rates in the United States: 1995.*
9. Garnier et al., "The Process of Dropping Out of High School."
   John Eckenrode et al., "School Performance and Disciplinary Problems Among Abused and Neglected Children," *Development Psychology* 29, no. 1 (1993): 53–62.
   Rowe and Eckenrode," The Timing of Academic Difficulties."
   Jeffrey Leiter and Matthew C. Johnsen, "Child Maltreatment and School Performance," *American Journal of Education* 102 no. 2 (1994): 54–89
   Dropout Rates in the United States: 1995.
10. Judy Mann, "A Perilous Age for Girls," *Washington Post*, 10 October 1997, sec. E, p. 3.
    The Commonwealth Fund Survey of the Health of Adolescent Girls, conducted by Louis Harris & Associates, ed. Cathy Schoen et al. (New York: The Commonwealth Fund, 1997).
11. Douglas Kirby, *No Easy Answers: Research Findings on Programs to Reduce Teen Pregnancy* (Washington, DC: The National Campaign to Prevent Teen Pregnancy, 1997).
    J. Manlove, *Breaking the Cycle of Disadvantage: Ties Between Educational Attainments, Dropping Out and School-Age Motherhood* (Washington, DC: Child Trends Inc., 1995).
    Garnier et al., "The Process of Dropping Out."
    National Mental Health Organization, *Children's and Adolescents' Mental Health* (factsheet) (Washington, DC, 1997).
    David Huizinga et al., *Urban Delinquency and Substance Abuse* (Washington, DC: U.S. Department of Justice, Office of Juvenile Justice and Delinquency Prevention, 1994).
12. Jessica Portner, "Hispanic Teenagers Top Black, White Birthrate," *Education Week* 17, no. 24 (February 25, 1998): 5.
13. Claire Brindiz and Susan Philliber, "Room to Grow. Improving Services for

Pregnant and Parenting Teenagers in School Settings," *Education and Urban Society* 30, no. 2 (1998): 242–260.

14. Laurence Steinberg, *Adolescence*, 4th ed. (New York: McGraw Hill, 1996). LaRue Allen et al., "Acculturation and Depression Among Latina Urban Girls," chapter 18 in *Urban Girls: Resisting Stereotypes, Creating Identities*, eds., Bonnie J. Ross Leadbeater and Niobe Way (New York: New York University Press, 1996): 337–352.

15. Ibid.

16. Department of Health and Human Services, Office of Applied Studies, Substance Abuse and Mental Health Services Administration, *Substance Use Among Women in the United States* (Washington, DC, 1997).
Girls with previous academic difficulties (e.g. poor grades, grade retentions) were more likely to become pregnant, use drugs and alcohol, and engage in delinquent behavior (Manlove, 1995; Kirby, 1997; Earle, 1989).

17. Garnier et al., "The Process of Dropping Out."
Substance Use Among Women in the United States.

18. *Hostile Hallways: The AAUW Survey on Sexual Harrassment in America's Schools*, (Washington, DC: American Association of University Women Educational Foundation, June 1993): 7, 11.

19. Ibid., 15.

20. Lynn Phillips, *The Girls Report: What We Know & Need to Know About Growing Up Female* (New York: The National Council for Research on Women, 1998): 49.

21. There are several caveats to bear in mind when interpreting this exhibit: (1) different sources and, thus, different samples were used; (2) studies collected information from different age ranges of students; (3) studies occurred in different years; (4) studies used different measures of risk (ever vs. past year vs. past month); and (5) studies employed different data collection procedures (self-report vs. transcripts).

22. Debra Schultz, *Risk, Resililiency, and Resistance: Current Research on Adolescent Girls* (New York: National Council for Research on Women, 1991): 6.

23. Nitza M. Hidalgo et al., "Research on Families, Schools, Communities: A Multicultural Perspective," *Academic Achievement: Approaches, Theories, and Research* (1995): 498–524.

24. Serge Madhere and Douglas J. Mac Iver, "Talent Development Middle School: Essential Components," Center for Research on the Education of Students Placed at Risk, Baltimore, MD. CRESPAR Newsletter, no. 1 (October 1996).

25. Sally M. Reis and Eva Diaz, "Economically Disadvantaged Urban Female Students Who Achieve in Schools," *Urban Education* (in press).
Jill McLean Taylor et al., *Between Voice and Silence: Women and Girls, Race and Relationship* (Cambridge: Harvard University Press, 1995).

Bonnie J. Ross Leadbeater and Niobe Way, *Urban Girls: Resisting Stereotypes, Creating Identities* (New York: New York University Press, 1996).

26. Adele R. Arellano and Amado M. Padilla, "Academic Invulnerability Among a Select Group of Latino University Students," *Hispanic Journal of Behavioral Sciences* 18, no. 4 (1996): 485–507.

27. Shwu-yong L. Huang and Hersholt C. Waxman, "Learning Environment Differences Between High- and Low-Achieving Minority Students in Urban Middle Schools" (paper presented at the annual meeting of the American Educational Research Association, New York, April 8–12, 1996).
   Shwu-yong L. Huang and Hersholt C. Waxman, "Motivation and Learning Environment Differences in Inner-City Middle School Students," *Journal of Educational Research* 90, no. 2 (1996): 93–102.

28. Janie V. Ward, "Cultivating a Morality of Care in African American Adolescents: A Cutlure Based Model of Violence Prevention, *Harvard Educational Review* 65, no. 2 (Summer 1995): 175.

29. Michael Rutter, "Stress, Coping, and Development: Some Issues and Some Questions," *Journal of Child Psychology and Psychiatry and Allied Disciplines* 24, no. 4 (1981): 323–356.
   Reis and Diaz, "Economically Disadvantaged Urban Female Students."
   Ibid., 6.

30. Robert Rossi and Samuel C. Stringfield, *Education Reform and Students At Risk* (Washington, DC: U.S. Department of Education, Office of Educational Research and Improvement,Natioanal Center for Educational Statistics, 1997).
   Susan Batten and Bonita Stowell, *School-Based Programs for Adolescent Parents and Their Young Children: Guidelines for Quality and Best Practice* (Bala Cynwyd, PA: Center for Assessment and Policy Development, 1996).
   The D.A.R.E. Program: A Review of Prevalence, User Satisfaction, and Effectiveness (Washington, DC: National Institute of Justice, 1994).
   Nan Stein, "Sexual Harassment in School: The Public Performance of Gendered Violence," *Harvard Educational Review* 65, no. 2 (1995): 145–162.

31. National Center for Health Statistics, in *Facts At A Glance* (Washington, DC: Child Trends, Inc., 1997).

32. Portner, "Hispanic Teenagers," 5.

33. Kirby, *No Easy Answers.*

34. Ibid.
   Judith Havemann, "Simply Preaching Abstinence Doesn't Cut Teen Pregnancy, Experts Say," *Washington Post,* 24 March 1997, sec. A, p. 7.

35. Kristin Luker, *Dubious Conceptions: The Politics of Teenage Pregnancy.* (Cambridge: Harvard University Press, 1996).
   Kirby, *No Easy Answers.*

36. Kirby, *No Easy Answers*.
37. Luker, *Dubious Conceptions*.
    Kirby, *No Easy Answers*.
38. *Programmed Neglect: Not Seen, Not Heard*, (New York: Ms. Foundation for Women, National Girls Initiative, October 1993).
39. Stein, "Sexual Harassment in School," 145–162.
40. The Empower Program. *Report*, Empower Program Class Descriptions. (Washington, DC: 1998).
41. *Title IX at 25: Report Card on Gender Equity*, (Washington, DC: National Coalition for Women and Girls in Education, 1997): 33.
42. Nan Stein, Nancy Marshall, and Linda Tropp, *Secrets in Public: Sexual Harassment in Our Schools* (Washington, DC and Wellesley, Mass.: NOW Legal Defense and Education Fund and Wellesley College Center for Women, 1993).
43. *Title IX at 25: Report Card on Gender Equity*, (Washington, DC: National Coalition for Women and Girls in Education, 1997).
    Delaine Eastin, *Pregnant and Parenting Student Programs: A Report to the Legislature* (Sacramento CA: California Department of Education, 1996).
    Batten and Stowell, *School-Based Programs for Adolescent Parents*.

Chapter Five

1. U.S. Department of Education, Office of Educational Research and Improvement, National Center for Education Statistics, *Extracurricular Participation and Student Engagement* (Washington, DC, 1995).
2. S.D. Lamborn et al., "Putting School in Perspective: The Influence of Family, Peers, Extracurricular Participation, and Part-Time Work on Academic Engagement," in *Student Engagement and Achievement in American Secondary Schools* (Washington, DC: U.S. Department of Education, Office of Educational Research and Improvement, National Center for Education Statistics, 1995).
   J.D. Finn, *School Engagement and Students at Risk* (Washington, DC: U.S. Department of Education, Office of Educational Research and Improvement, National Center for Education Statistics, 1993).
3. U.S. Department of Education, National Center for Education Statistics, Digest of Education Statistics 1996, NCES 96–133, by Thomas Snyder, Washington, DC: 1996, p. 137.
4. Ibid.
5. *Extracurricular Participation and Student Engagement*.
6. Ibid.
7. *Empowering Women in Sports*, The Empowering Women Series, no. 4 (Washington, DC: Feminist Majority Foundation, 1995).

8. *Title IX at 25: Report Card on Gender Equity* (Washington, DC: National Coalition for Women and Girls in Education, 1997).
   Don Sabo, *Gender Equity Report* (East Meadow, NY: Women's Sports Foundation, 1997).
9. *Title IX at 25: Report Card on Gender Equity.*
10. Sabo, *Gender Equity Report.*
    Women's Sports Facts (East Meadow, NY: Women's Sports Foundation, 1997).
11. Sabo, *Gender Equity Report.*
12. Linda K. Bunker et al., *The President's Council on Physical Fitness and Sports Report: Physical Activity and Sport in the Lives of Girls* (Washington, DC: President's Council on Physical Fitness and Sports, 1997).
    The 1996 High School Athletics Participation Survey (Kansas City, MO: The National Federation of State High School Associations, 1996).
13. *Empowering Women in Sports.*
14. Donna Lopiano, "Gender Equity and the Black Female in Sport" (excerpts from a presentation at the 5th annual Black Athletes in America Forum, Howard University, Washington, DC, April 9, 1993).
15. Bunker et al., *The President's Council.*
16. *The 1997 High School Athletics Participation Survey* (Kansas City, MO: The National Federation of State High School Associations, 1997).
    BW SportsWire (November 25, 1996), quoted in *Women's Sports Facts* (East Meadow, NY: Women's Sports Foundation, 1997).
17. Ibid.
18. Soccer Industry Council of America (1994), quoted in *Women's Sports Facts* (East Meadow, NY: Women's Sports Foundation, 1997).
19. Sally Ehlinger and Jennifer L. Katz, "Face-Off in Minnesota: A Pilot Study of Girls' Ice Hockey Experience During the First Year of State High School League-Sanctioned Play," *Melpomene* 14, no. 3 (1995): 22–26.
20. Pamela Manners and David Smart, "Moral Development and Identity Formation in High School Juniors: The Effects of Participation in Extracurricular Activities," paper presented at April 1995 annual meeting of American Educational Research Association, San Francisco, CA, ERIC Document ED385496; Donna Eder and David Kinney, "The Effects of Middle School Extracurricular Activities on Adolescents' Popularity and Peer Status," Youth and Society, 1995, vol. 26, #3, pp. 298–324; Constance Marie Webster, "It's Not Enough to Be Smart: Distinctions Among Female High School Peer Groups as They Narrate Their Gender Identity Construction in the Context of Extracurricular Activities," dissertation, 1997, State University of New York at Buffalo, Dissertation Abstracts Index, vol. 07A, p. 288.
21. Ibid.
22. Bunker et al., *The President's Council.*

Menopause, 3, no. 3 (1996): 172–180, quoted in *Women's Sports Facts* (East Meadow, NY: Women's Sports Foundation, 1997).

Leslie Bernstein et al., "Physical Exercise and Reduced Risk of Breast Cancer in Young Women," *Journal of the National Cancer Institute*, 86, no. 18 (September 21,1994): 1403–1408, quoted in *Women's Sports Facts* (East Meadow, NY: Women's Sports Foundation, 1997).

Teegarden and Proulx et al., *Medicine and Science in Sports and Exercise*, 28 (1996): 105–113, quoted in *Women's Sports Facts* (East Meadow, NY: Women's Sports Foundation, 1997).

23. Nicholas Zill et al., "The Life Circumstances and Development of Children in Welfare Families: A Profile Based on National Survey Data" (Washington, DC: Child Trends, 1991).

    Nicholas Zill et al., "Adolescent Time Use, Risky Behavior, and Outcomes: An Analysis of National Data" (Rockville, MD: Westat, Inc., 1995).

24. *Sporting Chance Program Series*, (New York: Girls, Inc., 1997): 1.

25. Sandra L. Hanson and Rebecca S. Kraus, "Women, Sports, and Science: Do Female Athletes Have an Advantage?" *Sociology of Education*, vol. 71, #2, April 1998, pp. 93–110.

26. *Title IX at 25: Report Card on Gender Equity* (Washington, DC: National Coalition for Girls and Women in Education 1997).

27. Research for Action, Inc., Jody Cohen and Sukey Blanc et al., *Girls in the Middle: Working to Succeed in School* (Washington, DC: American Association of University Women Educational Foundation, August, 1996): 70–71.

28. Lynn Phillips, *The Girls Report: What We Know & Need to Know About Growing Up Female* (New York: The National Council for Research on Women, 1998).

    Women and Girls in Sports (Washington, DC: Feminist Majority Foundation and New Media Publishing, Inc., 1995).

29. Barrie Thorne, *Gender Play: Girls & Boys in School* (New Brunswick, NJ: Rutgers University Press, 1993).

30. Nancy Theberge, "Gender, Sport, and the Construction of Community: A Case Study From Women's Ice Hockey," *Sociology of Sport Journal* 12, no. 4 (1995): 389–402.

31. Jay J. Coakley, *Sport in Society: Issues and Controversies* (New York: WCB/McGraw-Hill, 1998): 221.

32. G. Gross, "Girls Gleefully Claim a League of Their Own," *New York Times*, 4 August 1997, sec. A, p. 1.

33. *Title IX at 25: Report Card on Gender Equity.*

34. *Women and Girls in Sports.*

35. Lynn Jaffee and Rebecca Manzer, "Girls Perspectives: Physical Activity and Self-Esteem," *Melpomene Journal* 11, no. 3 (1992): 14–23.

36. Lynn Jaffee and Sherri Ricker, "Physical Activity and Self-Esteem in Girls: The Teen Years," *Melpomene Journal* 12, no. 3 (1993): 19–26.

37 *Empowering Women in Sports.*
    Title IX at 25.
38. Linda K. Bunker et al., *The President's Council on Physical Fitness and Sports Report: Physical Activity and Sport in the Lives of Girls.*
    Women and Girls in Sports.
    Carol Krucoff, "Sports Help Girls Navigate Through Teen Years," *Washington Post,* 22 April 1997, Health Section, p. 20.
39. Lynn Phillips, *The Girls Report: What We Know & Need to Know About Growing Up Female* (New York: The National Council for Research on Women, 1998): 18.
40. Coakley, *Sport in Society,* 212.
41. Beverly Sklover, "Women and Sports: The 25th Anniversery of Title IX," *Outlook* 90, no. 4 (1997): 13.
42. *Extracurricular Participation and Student Engagement.*
43. U.S. Department of Education and National Center for Education Statistics Office of Educational Research and Improvement, *Youth Indicators 1996* (Washington, DC: 1996): 92.
44. Ibid., 92.
45. Linda K. Bunker et al., *The President's Council on Physical Fitness and Sports Report: Physical Activity and Sports in the Lives of Girls* (Washington, DC: President's Council on Physical Fitness and Sports, 1997).
46. *Extracurricular Participation and Student Engagement.*
47. Alan R. Shoho and Irene T. Petrisky, "The Rural School Environment and Its Effect on Adolescent Alienation" (paper presented at the annual meeting of the American Educational Research Association, New York, April 8–12, 1996).
48. Susan B. Gerber, "Extracurricular Activities and Academic Performance," *Journal of Research and Development in Education* 30, no. 1 (Fall 1996): 42–50.
49. Kelly Ward, "Service-Learning and Student Volunteerism: Reflections on Institutional Commitment" (paper presented at the annual meeting of the American Educational Research Association, New York, April 8–12, 1996).
50. Ibid.
51. Pat Hutchinson and Tom Hughes, "Play Spaces: Linkages for Teaching, Learning and Service Project Links," *Technology Teacher* 56, no. 3 (1996): 31–33.
    Alan Haskitz, "A Community Service Program That Can Be Validated," *Phi Delta Kappan* 78, no. 2 (1996): 163–64.
    Miranda Yates and James Youniss, "Community Service and Political-Moral Identity in Adolescents," *Journal of Research on Adolescence* 6, no. 3 (1996): 271–84.
52. Jennifer Ocif and Beverly Marshall-Goodell, "Combining Mentoring and Service Learning" (paper presented at the National Conference of the Women in Engineering Program Advocates Network, June 1996).
53. J. Bachman and J. Schulenberg, "How Part-Time Work Intensity Relates to Drug Use, Problem Behavior, Time Use, and Satisfaction Among High School Seniors:

Are These Consequences or Merely Correlates?" *Developmental Psychology* 29 (1993) 2: 220–235. L. Steinberg et al., "Negative Impact of Part-Time Work on Adolescent Adjustment: Evidnece From a Longitudinal Study," *Developmental Psychology* 29 (1993) 2: 171–180.

54. Katherine S. Newman, "Working Poor: Low-Wage Employment in the Lives of Harlem Youth," in *Transitions Through Asolescence: Interpersonal Domains and Contexts*, ed. By Julie Graber et al. (Mahwah, NJ: Lawrence Erlbaum Associates, 1996): 332, 339.

55. Ibid., 332, 339.

Chapter Six

1. Helen S. Farmer, "Gender Differences in Adolescent Career Exploration," (Department of Labor, Office of Educational Research, 1995). *College-Bound Seniors: A Profile of SAT Program Test Takers* (New York: College Entrance Examination Board and Educational Testing Service, 1997): 8.

2. U.S. Department of Labor, Women's Bureau, *Labor Force Quiz* (Washington, DC, 1996).Careers are, in fact, classified as "nontraditional" when women comprise 25 percent or less of the total workers employed.

3. Sandra Kerka, "Trends and Issue Alerts: Gender Equity in Vocational Education," *ERIC Digests ED358376* (ERIC Clearinghouse on Alert, Career, and Vocational Education, Columbus, OH, 1993).

4. *Counselors' Role in the School-to-Work Opportunities Act of 1994* (Alexandria, VA: American School Counselors Association, 1995).

5. Anne Chapman, *A Great Balancing Act* (Washington, DC: National Association of Independent Schools, 1997).

6. Rosser, *Re-Engineering Female Friendly Science*.

7. Cheryl G. Bartholomew and Donna L. Schnorr, "Gender Equity: Suggestions for Broadening Career Options of Female Students," *The School Counselor* 41 (1994): 246.

8. Public Law 103–239, *School to Work Opportunities Act of 1994*, 4 May 1994.

9. Preliminary aggregated data indicate that of 707,472 secondary students enrolled in School-to-Work programs, 69 percent are white, 11 percent are Hispanic, 1 percent are Native American/Alaskan Native, and 4 percent are Asian/Pacific Islander. For a subsample of twelfth graders involved in intensive STW activities, additional data were reported. Race/ethnicity characteristics resemble those for the larger sample, and 46 percent were female (slightly lower than the percentage of females enrolled in school), 2 percent had limited English proficiency, 10 percent were categorized as students with disabilities, 22 percent as economically/educationally disadvantaged and 5 percent as academically gifted and talented.

10. Mary Wiberg, "The School-to-Work Opportunities Act: An Opportunity to Serve All Students." *Women's Educational Equity Act Publishing Center Digest* (Newton, MA, 1995).

11. Donna Milgram and Kristin Watkins, "Wider Opportunities for Women: Ensuring Quality School-To-Work Opportunities For Young Women" (Washington, DC: Wider Opportunities for Women, 1994).

12. Sue V. Rosser and Charlotte Hogsett, "Gender Equity in the School-to-Work Movement," in *Re-Engineering Female Friendly Science* (New York: Teachers College Press, 1997): 75.

    M. Dinsmore, *Washington State School to Work Opportunities System: Final Report to the Governor* (Olympia, WA: Governor's Council on School to Work, 1994), quoted in Rosser, *Re-Engineering Female Friendly Science.*

13. Despite the lack of generalizable or national data on STW, several STW projects directed specifically at girls have been instigated and are ongoing. One example is the Institute for Women in Trades, Technology and Science (IWITTS), which recently received a $100,000 National Science Foundation grant to design a training video for teachers on recruiting, retaining and preparing young women for careers in science, engineering, and mathematics through STW system building. An intensive train-the-teacher model will be used with both teachers and counselors in order to reach as many teachers as possible. An infrastructure to support gender equity is uneven, but in place. In 1995, the Council of Chief State School Officers surveyed individual states in their *early* efforts to provide supports to involve all students in school-to-work opportunities. Partee states that, the information presented is intended to be used as a baseline for measuring progress as a system development continues through the 1990s, In the report, 17 of the 47 states education agencies reported on planned or had in place strategies that were specific to the student groups described in the survey. Responses that could be categorized included students supports, technical assisstance, collaboration and partnership activities, comprehensive strategies and Federal and state programs and policies.

14. U.S. Department of Education, Office of Educational Research and Improvement, National Center for Education Statistics, *Study of School-to-Work Initiatives: Studies of Education Reform* (Washington, DC, 1996).

    Rachel Pedraza et al., *Home Grown Progress: The Evolution of Innovative School-to-Work Programs* (New York: Manpower Demonstration Research Corporation, 1997).

15. U.S. Department of Education, *Study of School-to-Work Initiatives.*

16. Pedraza, et al. *Home Grown Progress.*

17. Lynn Olson, *The School to Work Revolution: How Employers and Educators are Joining Forces to Prepare Tomorrow's Skilled Workforce* (Boston: Addison-Wesley, 1997).

18. Jenny L. Erwin, "Models For Serving All Students" *Women's Educational Equity Act Digest* (Newton, MA, 1995).

19. Sally M. Reis and M. Katherine Gavin, *Why Jane Doesn't Think She Can Do Math: How Teachers Can Encourage Talented Girls in Mathematics* (Reston, VA: National Council of Teachers of Mathematics, in press).

    Glenda Partee, *Ensuring All Students Access to School-to-Work Opportunity Systems in the States* (Washington, DC: Council of Chief State School Officers, 1995).

20. Donald E. Super, "A Life-Span, Life Space Approach to Career Development," in *Career Choice and Development*, 2nd ed. (San Francisco: Jossey-Bass, 1990).

    Farmer, "Gender Differences."

21. Esmerelda Cunanan and Carolyn M. Maddy-Bernstein, "The Role of the School Counselor" (Washington, DC: U.S. Department of Education, a brief from the Office of Special Populations).

22. *College-Bound Seniors: A Profile of SAT Program Test Takers* (New York: College Entrance Examination Board and Educational Testing Service, 1997): 8.

    The High School Profile Report (Iowa City, IA: American College Testing Program, 1990–1997).

23. Karen Arnold, *Lives of Promise: What Becomes of High School Valedictorians, A 14 Year Study of Achievement and Life Choices* (San Francisco: Jossey-Bass, 1995): 292.

24. Ofra Nevo, "Career Counseling from the Counselee Perspective: Analysis of Feedback Questionnaires," *The Career Development Quarterly* 38, no. 4 (June 1990): 314–324.

25. Norman C. Gysbers and Patricia Henderson, *Developing and Managing Your School Guidance Program*, 2nd ed. (Alexandria, VA: American Association for Counseling and Development, 1994).

26. Farmer, "Gender Differences."

27. Ibid.

28. Suzanne Silverman and Alice Pritchard, "Guidance, Gender Equity and Technology Education," *ERIC Digests*, ED362651 (Washington, DC, 1993).

29. Ibid.

    Suzanne Silverman and Alice Pritchard, *Building Their Future: Girls in Technology Education in Connecticut* (Hartford: Vocational Equity Research, Training and Evaluation Center, 1993b).

30. Rosser and Hogsett, "Gender Equity in the School-to-Work Movement," 77.

    Rosser, *Re-Engineering Female Friendly Science.*

31. Ibid.

32. Milgram and Watkins, *Ensuring Quality School-to-Work Opportunities.*

33. Patricia B. Campbell and Karen Steinbrueck, *Striving for Gender Equity: National Programs to Increase Student Engagement with Math and Science* (Washington, DC: Collaboration for Equity, Fairness in Science and Mathematics Education, 1996).

34. Bartholomew and Schnorr, "Gender Equity," 246.

35. Jill McLean Taylor et al., *Between Voice and Silence: Women and Girls, Race and Relationship* (Cambridge: Harvard University Press, 1995): 174–176.

Chapter Seven

1. Jeff Archer, "Surge in Hispanic Student Enrollment Predicted," *Education Week* 15, no. 27 (March 27, 1996): 1.

   U.S. Department of Education, Office of Educational Research and Improvement, National Center for Education Statistics, *Digest of Education Statistics 1996* (Washington, DC, 1996): 96–133.

   U.S. Department of Education, Office of Bilingual Education and Minority Languages Affairs, *No More Excuses: The Final Report of the Hispanic Dropout Project* (Washington, DC, February 1998).

   Kathleen Vail, "Keeping Fernando in School: In Denver, a Bold Approach is Stemming the Tide of Hispanic Dropouts," *The American School Board Journal* (February 1998): 33.

   Ines Pinto Alicea, "No More Excuses; the Time to Act is Now: Scholars Release Report on Dropout Rate," *Hispanic Outlook in Higher Education* 8, no. 2 (September 19, 1997): 6.

2. Kathleen Vail, "Keeping Fernando," 31.

   Gustavo A. Mellander, "College-Bound Hispanics: Marking the Path," *Hispanic Outlook in Higher Education* 8, no. 12 (February 13, 1998): 4.

   Angela McGlynn, "Hispanic Women, Academia and Retention," *Hispanic Outlook in Higher Education* 8, no. 12 (February 13, 1998).

   Rosa Maria Gil, *The Maria Paradox: How Latins Can Merge Old World Traditions with New World Self Esteem* (New York: GP Putnam's Sons, 1996).

   Sarah Cooke, "Why Hispanic-American Women Succeed in Higher Education," editorial, *Women in Higher Education* 7, no. 2 (February 1998): 8.

3. Elaine Woo, "School Success of Immigrants' Children Tracked," *Los Angeles Times*, 16 June 1997, sec. A.

   Vivien Lee and Rachel Sing, "Gender Equity in Schools for Immigrant Girls," *New Voices, Newsletter from the National Center for Immigrant Students* 3, no. 2 (1993): 1.

   Debra Viadero, "Immigrant Children Succeed Despite Barriers," *Education Week* 7, no. 29 (April 1, 1998): 14.

4. Sondra Cooney, "Education's Weak Link: Student Performance in the Middle Grades," *Southern Regional Education Board* (1998).

5. Eric Wee, "Turning to Teenagers for Tech Talent," *Washington Post*, 1 March 1998, sec. A, p.1.

6. Mary Ann Zehr, "Computer Giants Look to Students: Companies Setting Up Certification Programs," *Education Week* 17, no. 31 (April 15, 1998): 1.

7. Larry Leslie et al., "Women and Minorities in Science and Engineering: A Life Sequence Analysis," *The Journal of Higher Education* 69, no. 3 (May/June 1998): 268.

8. Maxine Greene, *Releasing the Imagination: Essays on Education, the Arts and Social Change* (San Francisco: Jossey-Bass, 1995): 9.

    Karen Ferneding Lenert, "Reform Policy and the 'Inevitable' Diffusion of Electronic Technology: Reclaiming Teachers' Voices Through Building a Diverse Community of Discourse," (paper presented at the American Educational Research Association annual meeting, San Diego, CA, 1998), 14.

9. Jeffrey Selingo, "Task Force Suggests that University of California Drop SAT as Admissions Requirement," *The Chronicle of Higher Education* 3 October 1997, sec. A, p. 37.

    Patrick Healy, "University of California Weighs Admitting Top 4% of Students from Each High School," *The Chronicle of Higher Education* 6 March 1998, sec. A, p. 37.

    Nancy Cole, "Gender and Fair Assessment," (paper presented at the American Educational Research Association, San Diego, CA, 1998).

10. Priscilla Wohlstetter, et al., "First Lessons: Charter Schools as Learning Communities," *CPRE Policy Briefs* (September, 1997): 1.

    Dan Goldhaber, "School Choice as Education Reform," *Phi Delta Kappan* 79, no. 2 (October 1997): 143.

    Linda Jacobson, "Under the Microscope: Charter Schools," *Education Week* 16, no. 10 (November 6, 1996): 21–23.

11. Geoff Whitty, "Creating Quasi-Markets in Education," Michael Apple, ed., *Review of Research in Education*, 22 (AERA: 1997): 1–47.

    Mark Walsh, "Commercial Invasion of Schools Growing, Report Charges," *Education Week* 14, no. 31 (April 26, 1995): 6.

BIBLIOGRAPHY

Alicea, Ines Pinto, "No More Excuses; the Time to Act is Now: Scholars Release Report on Dropout Rate," *Hispanic Outlook in Higher Education* 8, no. 2 (September 19, 1997): 6

Allen, LaRue, et al., "Acculturation and Depression Among Latina Urban Girls," chapter 18 in *Urban Girls: Resisting Stereotypes, Creating Identities*, eds., Bonnie J. Ross Leadbeater and Niobe Way (New York: New York University Press, 1996): 337–352.

An Independent Evaluation of the Kentucky Instructional Results Information System (KIRIS) (Frankfort, KY: Kentucky Institute for Education Research, 1995).

Archer, Jeff, "Surge in Hispanic Student Enrollment Predicted," *Education Week* 15, no. 27 (March 27, 1996): 3.

Arellano, Adele R. and Amado M. Padilla, "Academic Invulnerability Among a Select Group of Latino University Students," *Hispanic Journal of Behavioral Sciences* 18, no. 4 (1996): 485–507.

Arnold, Karen, *Lives of Promise: What Becomes of High School Valedictorians, A 14 Year Study of Achievement and Life Choices* (San Francisco: Jossey-Bass, 1995): 292.

Assessment Standards for School Mathematics (Reston, VA: National Council for Teachers of Mathematics, 1995).

Astin, Alexander and Helen S. Astin, *Undergraduate Science Education: The Impact of Different College Environments on the Educational Pipeline in the Sciences* (Los Angeles: Higher Education Research Institute, University of California, 1993).

Bachman, J. and J. Schulenberg, "How Part-Time Work Intensity Relates to Drug Use, Problem Behavior, Time Use, and Satisfaction Among High School Seniors: Are These Consequences or Merely Correlates?" *Developmental Psychology* 29 (1993) 2: 220–235.

Bailey, Susan M., "The Current Status of Gender Equity Research in American Schools," *Educational Psychologist* 24, no. 4 (1993): 321–339.

Bailey, Susan M. and Patricia B. Campbell, "Gender Equity: The Unexamined Basic of School Reform," *Stanford Law and Policy Review* (1992): 73–86.

Bank, Barbara J. and Peter M. Hall, eds. *Gender, Equity and Schooling: Policy and Practice*, Missouri Symposium on Research and Educational Policy, vol. 2 (New York: Garland Publishing, Inc., 1997).

Bartholomew, Cheryl G. and Donna L. Schnorr, "Gender Equity: Suggestions for Broadening Career Options of Female Students," *The School Counselor* 41 (1994): 246.

Batten, Susan and Bonita Stowell, *School-Based Programs for Adolescent Parents and Their Young Children: Guidelines for Quality and Best Practice* (Bala Cynwyd, PA: Center for Assessment and Policy Development, 1996).

Beaton, Albert E., et al., *Science Achievement in the Middle School Years: IEA's Third International Mathematics and Science Study, (TIMSS)* (Chestnut Hill, MA: Center for the Study of Testing, Evaluation, and Educational Policy, Boston College, 1997).

Beck, Irene, "Gender Equity in Schools: Beyond Sugar and Spice," *PTA Today* 20 (Jan–Feb 1995): 11–13.

Bendixen-Noe, Mary K. and Lynne Degler Hall, "The Quest for Gender Equity in America's Schools: From Preschool and Beyond," *Journal of Early Childhood Teacher Education* 17, no. 2 (1996): 50–57.

Bernstein, Leslie, et al., "Physical Exercise and Reduced Risk of Breast Cancer in Young Women," *Journal of the National Cancer Institute* 86, no. 18 (September 21, 1994): 1403–1408, quoted in *Women's Sports Facts* (East Meadow, NY: Women's Sports Foundation, 1997).

Berube, Maurice R., "The Politics of National Standards," *The Clearing House* 69, no. 3 (1996): 151–153.

Beyer, Christine E., "Gender Representation in Illustrations, Text and Topic Areas in Sexuality Education Curricula," *Journal of School Health* 66 (December 1996): 361–64.

Blank, Rolf K. et al., *Mathematics and Science Content Standards and*

Curriculum Frameworks: State Progress on Development and Implementation (Washington, DC: Council of Chief State School Officers, 1997).

Blank, Rolf and Doreen Gruebel, *State Indicators of Science and Mathematics Education: State by State Trends and New Indicators from the 1993-1994 School Year* (Washington, DC: Council of Chief State School Officers, 1995).

Braddock II, Jomills Henry and Robert E. Slavin, "Why Ability Grouping Must End: Achieving Excellence and Equity in American Education," *Beyond Tracking: Finding Success in Inclusive Schools,* eds., H. Pool and J. A. Page (Bloomington: Phi Delta Kappa Educational Foundation, 1995): 7–20.

Brindiz, Claire and Susan Philliber, "Room to Grow. Improving Services for Pregnant and Parenting Teenagers in School Settings," *Education and Urban Society* 30, no. 2 (1998): 242–260.

Brunner, Cornelia, associate director, Educational Development Center, in a personal letter to Pamela Haag, senior research associate, January 7, 1998, American Association of University Women Educational Foundation, Washington, DC.

Bunker, Linda K., et al., *The President's Council on Physical Fitness and Sports Report: Physical Activity and Sports in the Lives of Girls* (Washington, DC: President's Council on Physical Fitness and Sports, 1997).

Burkham, David T., et al., "Gender and Science Learning Early in High School: Subject Matter and Laboratory Experiences," *American Educational Research Journal* 34, no. 2 (1997): 297–331.

BW SportsWire (November 25, 1996), quoted in *Women's Sports Facts* (East Meadow, NY: Women's Sports Foundation, 1997).

Campbell, Jay R., et al., *NAEP 1996 Trends in Academic Progress* (Washington, DC: U. S. Department of Education, Office of Educational Research and Improvement, National Center for Education Statistics, 1997).

Campbell, Patricia B. and Jo Sanders, "Uninformed But Interested: Findings of a National Survey on Gender Equity in Preservice Teacher Education," *Journal of Teacher Education* 48, no. 1 (1997): 69–75.

Campbell, Patricia B. and Karen Steinbrueck, *Striving for Gender Equity: National Programs to Increase Student Engagement with Math and Science* (Washington, DC: Collaboration for Equity, Fairness in Science and Mathematics Education, 1996).

Campbell, Patricia B., and Ellen Wahl, "What's Sex Got to Do With It? Simplistic Questions, Complex Answers," in *Separated by Sex: A*

Critical Look at Single-Sex Education for Girls (Washington, DC: American Association of University Women Educational Foundation, March 1998): 70.

Carey, Deborah A., et al., "Equity and Mathematics Education," in *New Directions for Equity in Mathematics Education*, eds. Walter G. Secada, et al. (Cambridge: Harvard University Press, 1995): 93–125.

Caseau, D. L., et al., "Special Education Services for Girls with Serious Emotional Disturbance: A Case of Gender Bias?," *Behavorial Disorders* 20, no.1 (1994): 51–60.

Casey, M. Beth and Patricia Howson, "Educating Preservice Students Based on a Problem-Centered Approach to Teaching," *Journal of Teacher Education* 44, no. 5 (1993): 361–69.

Chapman, Anne, *A Great Balancing Act: Equitable Education for Girls and Boys* (National Association of Independent Schools, 1997).

Chenowith, Karen, "A Measurement of What?" Black Issues in Higher Education 14, no. 14 (1997) 14: 18–22.

Chepyator-Thomson, Rose Jepkorir and Catherine D. Ennis, "Reproduction and Resistance to the Culture of Femininity and Masculinity in Secondary School Physical Education," *Research Quarterly for Exercise and Sport* 68 (March 1997): 89–99.

Cleary, Theresa Anne, "Gender Differences in Aptitude and Achievement Test Scores," in *Sex Equity in Educational Opportunity, Achievement, and Testing: Proceedings of the 1991 ETS Invitational Conference* (Princeton, NJ: Educational Testing Service): 51–90.

Clewell, Beatriz Chu, et al., *Systemic Reform in Mathematics and Science Education: An Urban Perspective* (Washington, DC: The Urban Institute, 1995).

———. *Breaking the Barriers. Helping Female and University Students Succeed in Science* (San Francisco: Jossey-Bass, 1992).

Coakley, Jay J., *Sport in Society: Issues and Controversies* (New York: WCB/McGraw-Hill, 1998): 221.

Cohen, Jody and Sukey Blanc et al., *Girls in the Middle: Working to Succeed in School*, researched by Research for Action, Inc. (Washington, DC: American Association of University Women Educational Foundation, 1996).

Cole, Nancy, "Gender and Fair Assessment," (paper presented at the American Educational Research Association, San Diego, 1998).

Cole, Nancy and Warren W. Willingham, *Gender and Fair Assessment*, (Princeton: Educational Testing Service, Mahwah, NJ: Lawrence Erlbaum Associates, 1997): 122.

College-Bound Seniors: A Profile of SAT Program Test Takers (New York: College
Entrance Examination Board and Educational Testing Service
1997): 8.

Collins, James, "How Johnny Should Read, *Time* 150, no. 17 (October 27,
1997).

Computers and Classrooms: The Status of Technology in U.S. Schools
(Princeton, NJ: Educational Testing Service, 1997).

Cook, Sarah "Why Hispanic-American Women Succeed in Higher
Education," editorial, *Women in Higher Education* 7, no. 2
(February 1998): 8.

Cooney, Sondra, "Education's Weak Link: Student Performance in the
Middle Grades," *Southern Regional Education Board* (1998).

Counselors' Role in the School-to-Work Opportunities Act of 1994 (Alexandria,
VA: American School Counselors Association, 1995).

Crombie, Gail, et al., "Gifted Programs: Gender Differences in Referral and
Enrollment," *Gifted Child Quarterly* 36, no. 4 (1992): 212–213.

Cummings, Rebecca, "11th Graders View Gender Differences in Reading
and Math," *Journal of Reading* 38, no. 3 (November 1994):
196–99.

Cunanan, Esmerelda and Carolyn M. Maddy-Bernstein, "The Role of the
School Counselor" (Washington, DC: U.S. Department of
Education, Office of Special Populations).

D'Ambrosio, Melody and Patricia S. Hammer, "Gender Equity in the
Catholic Elementary Schools" (paper presented at the annual con-
vention and exposition of the National Catholic Education
Association, Philadelphia, April 1996).

Dauber, Susan L., et al., "Tracking and Transition through the Middle
Grades: Chanelling Educational Trajectories," *Sociology of Education*
69, no. 4: 290–307.

Davis, Cinda-Sue, et al., *The Equity Equation: Fostering the Advancement of
Women in the Sciences, Mathematics, and Engineering* (San Francisco:
Jossey-Bass, 1996).

Davis, Cinda-Sue and Sue V. Rosser, "Program and Curricular
Interventions," in *The Equity Equation*, eds. Cinda-Sue Davis et al.
(San Francisco: Jossey-Bass, 1996): 232–264.

Del Portillo, Ray and Margot M. Segura, foreword to *Cada cabeza es un
mundo/ Each Mind is a World*, by Jose Antonio Burciaga et al.
(Sausalito, CA: The California Latino-Chicano High School
Dropout Prevention Project, 1996).

Dinsmore, M., *Washington State School to Work Opportunities System: Final Report to the Governor* (Olympia, WA: Governor's Council on School to Work, 1994).

Draft Standards for Identifying and Supporting Quality Professional Development Schools (Washington, DC: National Council for Accreditation of Teacher Education, 1997).

Durham, Staci, and Sheila Brownlow, "Sex Differences in the Use of Science and Technology in Children's Cartoons," *Journal of Science Education and Technology* 6, no. 2 (June 1997): 103–110.

Eastin, Delaine, *Pregnant and Parenting Student Programs: A Report to the Legislature* (Sacramento, CA: California Department of Education, 1996).

Eckenrode, John, et al., "School Performance and Disciplinary Problems Among Abused and Neglected Children," *Development Psychology* 29, no. 1 (1993): 53–62.

Edwards, Virginia B., et al., "The Urban Challenge," *Education Week* 17, no. 17 (January 8, 1998): 6.

Ehlinger, Sally and Jennifer L. Katz, "Face-Off in Minnesota: A Pilot Study of Girls' Ice Hockey Experience During the First Year of State High School League-Sanctioned Play," *Melpomene* 14, no. 3 (1995): 22–26.

"Empowering Women in Sports," *The Empowering Women Series*, no. 4 (Washington, DC: Feminist Majority Foundation, 1995).

Entwisle, Doris R., et al., *Children, Schools, and Inequality*, Social Inequality Series (Boulder, CO: Westview Press, 1997).

Erwin, Jenny L., "Models For Serving All Students" *Women's Educational Equity Act Digest* (Newton, MA, 1995).

Facts At A Glance (Washington, DC: Child Trends, Inc., 1997).

Falk, Beverly and Linda Darling-Hammond, *The Primary Language Record at P. S. 261: How Assessment Transforms Teaching and Learning* (New York: National Center for Restructuring Education, Schools, and Teaching, 1993).

Farmer, Helen S., "Gender Differences in Adolescent Career Exploration," (Department of Labor, Office of Educational Research, 1995).

Fine, Michelle, et al., "Communities of Difference: A Critical Look at Desegregated Spaces Created to and by Youth," *Harvard Educational Review* 67, no. 2 (1997): 274–284.

Fine, Michelle, *Framing Dropouts: Notes on the Politics of an Urban High School* (Albany, NY: SUNY, 1990).

Finn, J.D., *School Engagement and Students at Risk* (Washington, DC: U.S. Department of Education, Office of Educational Research and Improvement, National Center for Education Statistics, 1993).

Fordham, Signithia, "Those Loud Black Girls: (Black) Women, Silence, and Gender Passing in the Academy," chapter 31 in *Anthropology and Education Quarterly* 24, no. 1 (1993): 3–32.

———. *Blacked Out: Dilemmas of Race, Identity, and Success at Capital High* (Chicago: The University of Chicago Press, 1996).

Foster, Michelle, "African American Teachers and Culturally Relevant Pedagogy," chapter 31 in *The Handbook of Research on Multicultural Education*, eds. James Banks and Cherry Banks (New York: Macmillan, 1995): 570–581.

Garnier, Helen Z., et al., "The Process of Dropping Out of High School: A 19-Year Perspective," *American Educational Research Journal* 34, no. 2 (1997): 397.

Garriques, George L., "National Merit Scholarships: A Major Dash of Jim Crow," *Journal of Blacks in Higher Education* 3 (Spring 1994), pp. 60–64.

Gerber, Susan B., "Extracurricular Activities and Academic Performance," *Journal of Research and Development in Education* 30, no. 1 (Fall 1996): 42–50.

Gil, Rosa Maria, *The Maria Paradox: How Latins Can Merge Old World Traditions with New World Self Esteem* (New York: GP Putnam's Sons, 1996).

Gilligan, Carol, *In a Different Voice: Psychological Theory and Women's Development* (Cambridge, MA: Harvard University Press, 1982).

Goldhaber, Dan, "School Choice as Education Reform," *Phi Delta Kappan* 79, no. 2 (October 1997): 143.

Gormley, Kathleen, et al., "Gender Differences In Classroom Writing: An Analysis of Sixth Grade Students' Reader Response Entries," *Eric Digests ED353578* (Washington, DC: Eric Clearinghouse, 1992).

Greene, Maxine, *Releasing the Imagination: Essays on Education, the Arts and Social Change* (San Francisco: Jossey-Bass, 1995): 9.

Greenfield, Teresa, "Girls and Boys Use of Interactive Science Museums (paper presented at the American Education Research Association meeting, San Francisco, 1995).

Grinder, Elizabeth and Pam Gordon, "Current Teacher Induction Practices in the United States" (background paper, Pelavin Research Institute, 1995).

Gross, G., "Girls Gleefully Claim a League of Their Own," *New York Times*, 4 August 1997, sec. A, p. 1.

Gurak, L. J. and N. L. Bayer, "Making Gender Visible: Extending Feminist Critiques of Technology to Technical Communication," *Technical Communication Quarterly* 3 (Summer 1994): 257–70.

Guthrie, Julian, "Book List Approval a Story of Passion, Negotiation," *San Francisco Examiner*, 23 March 1998, p. 1.

Gysbers, Norman C. and Patricia Henderson, *Developing and Managing Your School Guidance Program*, 2nd ed. (Alexandria, VA: American Association for Counseling and Development, 1994).

Halbrook, Arthur and Katherine Woodward, *National and State Content Standards in Enligh Language Arts* (Washington, DC: GED Testing Service, American Council on Education).

Hallinan, Maureen T., "School Differences in Tracking Effects on Achievement," *Social Forces* 72, no. 3 (March 1994): 799–820.

Halpern, "The Disappearance of Cognitive Gender Differences: What You See Depends on Where You Look," *American Psychology* 44, no. 8 (1989): 1156–1158.

Hansen, Sunny, et al., *Growing Smart: What's Working for Girls in School* (Washington, DC: American Association of University Women Educational Foundation, 1995).

Hanson, Sandra L., *Lost Talent: Women in the Sciences* (Philadelphia: Temple University Press, 1996).

Haskitz, Alan, "A Community Service Program That Can Be Validated," *Phi Delta Kappan* 78, no. 2 (1996): 163–64.

Havemann, Judith, "Simply Preaching Abstinence Doesn't Cut Teen Pregnancy, Experts Say," *Washington Post*, March 24, 1997, sec. A, p. 7.

Haworth, Karla, "Teacher-Education Accreditor Issues: Draft Standards for Training Programs," *The Chronicle of Higher Education* (October 1997).

Hayes, Elizabeth and Jennifer Hopkins, "Gender Literacy Learning: Implications for Research in Adult Literacy Education" (paper presented at the annual meeting of the American Educational Research Association (New York: April 1995).

Healy, Patrick, "University of California Weighs Admitting Top 4% of Students from Each High School," *The Chronicle of Higher Education* 6 March 1998, sec. A, p. 37.

Hidalgo, Nitza M., et al., "Research on Families, Schools, Communities: A Multicultural Perspective," in *Academic Achievement: Approaches, Theories, and Research* (1995): 502.

Hodes, Carol L., "Gender Representations in Mathematics Software," *Journal of Educational Technology Systems* 24, no. 1 (1995–96): 67–73.

Hollenshead, Carole S., "Exploring Explanations for Gender Differences in High School Students' Science Achievement" (remarks at the annual meeting of the American Educational Research Association, Chicago, March 24–28, 1997).

Honey, Margaret, *For the Maternal Voice in the Technological Universe* (paper presented at the Girls and Technology conference, Marymount University, Tarrytown, NY, 1997).

Horgan, Dianne D., *Achieving Gender Equity: Strategies for the Classroom* (Boston: Allyn & Bacon, 1995).

Hostile Hallways: The AAUW Survey on Sexual Harrassment in America's Schools, (Washington, DC: American Association of University Women Educational Foundation, June 1993): 7, 11.

How Schools Shortchange Girls: The AAUW Report, A Study of Major Findings on Girls and Education, researched by the Wellesley College Center for Research on Women (Washington, DC: American Association of University Women Educational Foundation, 1992; New York: Marlowe and Company, 1995).

Huang, Shwu-Yong L. and Hersholt C. Waxman, "Motivation and Learning Environment Differences in Inner-City Middle School Students," *Journal of Educational Research* 90, no. 2 (1996): 93–102.

———. "Learning Environment Differences Between High- and Low-Achieving Minority Students in Urban Middle Schools" (paper presented at the annual meeting of the American Educational Research Association, New York, April 8–12, 1996).

Hughes-McDonnell, F., *Understanding High School Physics Students Perspectives of Their Classroom Experiences and Their Images of Physics and Physicists: A Pilot Study* (Cambridge: Harvard Graduate School of Education, 1996).

Huizinga, David, et al., *Urban Delinquency and Substance Abuse* (Washington, DC: U.S. Department of Justice, Office of Juvenile Justice and Delinquency Prevention, 1994).

Humphrey, Daniel C. and Patrick M. Shields, *A Review of the Mathematics and Science Curriculum Frameworks* (Menlo Park, CA: SRI International, April 1996).

Hutchinson, Pat and Tom Hughes, "Play Spaces: Linkages for Teaching, Learning and Service Project Links," *Technology Teacher* 56, no. 3 (1996): 31–33.

Jacobson, Linda, "Under the Microscope: Charter Schools," *Education Week* 16, no. 10 (November 6, 1996): 21–23.

Jaffee, Lynn and Rebecca Manzer, "Girls Perspectives: Physical Activity and Self-Esteem," *Melpomene Journal* 11, no. 3 (1992): 14–23.

Jaffee, Lynn and Sherri Ricker, "Physical Activity and Self-Esteem in Girls: The Teen Years," *Melpomene Journal* 12, no. 3 (1993): 19–26.

Jerald, Craig D., et al., "The State of the States," *Education Week* 17, no. 17 (January 8, 1998): 76–89.

Jones, Jacqueline and Edward Chittenden, "An Observational Study of NBPTS Candidates As They Progress Through the Certification Process" (symposium at the annual meeting of the American Educational Research Association, Chicago, 1997).

Kahle, Jane B. and A. Damnjanovic, "The Effect of Inquiry Activities on Elementary Students Enjoyment, Ease, and Confidence in Doing Science: An Analysis by Sex and Race," *Journal of Women and Minorities in Science and Engineering* 1 (1994): 17–28.

Kahle, Jane B., "Opportunities and Obstacles: Science Education in the Schools," in *The Equity Equation: Fostering the Advancement of Women in the Sciences, Mathematics, and Engineering*, eds., Cinda-Sue Davis et al. (San Francisco: Jossey-Bass, 1996): 57–95.

―――. "What We Have Learned: A Reformed Researcher's Perspective" (paper prepared for the National Science Foundation, Grant #OSR-92500, n.d.).

Kahle, Jane B., and Judith Meece, "Research on Gender Issues in the Classroom," chapter 18 in *Handbook of Research in Science Teaching and Learning*, ed. Dorothy L. Gabel (New York: Macmillan, 1994).

Kane, Michael and Sol Pelavin, *Changing the Odds: Factors Increasing Access to College* (New York: The College Board, 1990).

Kerka, Sandra, "Trends and Issue Alerts: Gender Equity in Vocational Education," *Eric Digest ED358376* (ERIC Clearinghouse on Alert, Career, and Vocational Education, Columbus, OH, 1993).

Kirby, Douglas, *No Easy Answers: Research Findings on Programs to Reduce Teen Pregnancy* (Washington, DC: The National Campaign to Prevent Teen Pregnancy, 1997).

Klein, Stephen P., et al., "Gender and Racial/Ethnic Differences on Performance Assessments in Science," *Educational Evalution and Policy Analysis* 19, no. 2 (Summer 1997): 83

Koch, Melissa, "Opening up Technology to Both Genders," *Technos* 3 (1994): 14–19.

Kreinberg, Nancy and Ellen Wahl, eds. *Thoughts and Deeds: Equity in Mathematics and Science Education* (Washington, DC.: American Association for the Advancement of Science, Collaboration for Equity, 1997)

Krucoff, Carol, "Sports Help Girls Navigate Through Teen Years," *Washington Post*, April 22, 1997, Health Section, p. 20.

Ladson-Billings, Gloria, "Multicultural Teacher Education: Research Practice and Policy," chapter 43 in *The Handbook of Research on Multicultural Education*, eds James Banks and Cherry Banks (New York: Macmillan, 1995): 747–759.

Lamborn, S.D., et al., "Putting School in Perspective: The Influence of Family, Peers, Extracurricular Participation, and Part-Time Work on Academic Engagement," in *Student Engagement and Achievement in American Secondary Schools* (Washington, DC: U.S. Department of Education, Office of Educational Research and Improvement, National Center for Education Statistics, 1995).

Leadbeater, Bonnie J. Ross and Niobe Way, *Urban Girls: Resisting Stereotypes, Creating Identities* (New York: New York University Press, 1996).

Lee, Valerie E., "Gender Equity and the Organization of Schools," in *Gender, Equity and Schooling* (New York: Garland Publishing, Inc., 1997).

———. "Is Single-Sex Secondary Schooling a Solution to the Problem of Gender Inequity," in *Separated by Sex: A Critical Look at Single-Sex Education for Girls* (Washington, DC: American Association of University Women Educational Foundation, March 1998): 41–52.

Lee, Valerie E., et al., "Sexism in Single-Sex and Coeducational Independent Secondary School Classrooms," *Sociology of Education* 67, no. 2 (1994): 92–120.

Lee, Vivien and Rachel Sing, "Gender Equity in Schools for Immigrant Girls," *New Voices, Newsletter from the National Center for Immigrant Students* 3, no. 2 (1993): 1.

Leiter, Jeffrey and Matthew C. Johnsen, "Child Maltreatment and School Performance," *American Journal of Education* 102 no. 2 (1994): 54–89.

Lenert, Karen Ferneding, "Reform Policy and the 'Inevitable' Diffusion of Electronic Technology: Reclaiming Teachers' Voices Through Building a Diverse Community of Discourse," (paper presented at the American Educational Research Association annual meeting, San Diego, 1998).

Leslie, Larry, et al., "Women and Minorities in Science and Engineering: A Life Sequence Analysis," *The Journal of Higher Education* 69, no. 3 (May/June 1998): 268.

Linn, Marcia and Cathy Kessel, "Grades or Scores: Predicting Future College Mathematics Performance," *Educational Measurement: Issues and Practice* 15, no. 4 (Winter 1996): 10–14, 38.

Lopiano, Donna, "Gender Equity and the Black Female in Sport" (excerpts from a presentation at the 5th annual Black Athletes in America Forum, Howard University, Washington, DC, April 9, 1993).

Luker, Kristin, *Dubious Conceptions: The Politics of Teenage Pregnancy.* (Cambridge: Harvard University Press, 1996).

Madhere, Serge, and Douglas J. Mac Iver, "Talent Development Middle School: Essential Components," Center for Research on the Education of Students Placed at Risk, Baltimore, MD, CRESPAR Newsletter, no. 1 (October 1996).

Maher, Frances A., "Progressive Education and Feminist Pedagogy: Issues in Gender, Power, and Authority," in *Gender and Race on the Campus and in the School: Beyond Affirmative Action*, (Washington, DC: American Association of University Women, 1997).

Malcolm, S. M., "Science for All: Easy to Say, Hard to Do," in *In Pursuit of Excellence: National Standards for Science Education*, ed. A. Pendergast (proceedings of the AAAS Forum for School Science, Washington, DC, 1992).

Mangione, Melissa, "Understanding the Critics of Educational Technology: Gender Inequalities and Computers 1983–1993" (in proceedings of the 1995 annual national convention of the Association for Educational Communications and Technology (AECT) Anaheim, CA, 1995).

Manlove, J., *Breaking the Cycle of Disadvantage: Ties Between Educational Attainments, Dropping Out and School-Age Motherhood* (Washington, DC: Child Trends Inc., 1995).

Mann, Judy, "A Perilous Age for Girls," *Washington Post* Washington, DC, October 10, 1997, sec. E, p. 3.

Manzo, Kathleen Kennedy, "Glimmer of History Standards Show Up in Latest Textbooks," *Education Week* 17, no. 6 (October 8, 1997): 1, 11.

————. "For Girls, Writing's on the Wall in New PSAT Exam," *Education Week* 17, no. 20 (January 28, 1998).

Margolis, Jeannie and Alan Fisher, "Women in Computer Sciences: Closing the Gender Gap in Higher Education" (second annual report to the Sloan Foundation, Carnegie Mellon University School of Computer Science, Pittsburgh, 1997).

Marso, Ronald N. and Fred L. Pigge, "Teacher Mentor Induction Programs: An Assessment of First-Year Teachers" (paper presented at the annual meeting of the Association of Teacher Educators 70th Annual Conference, Las Vegas, Nevada, 1990).

Mathematics and Science Content Standards and Curriculum Frameworks: State Progress on Development and Implementation (Washington, DC: Council of Chief State School Officers, 1997).

McCall, Cecilia, "Gender and Reading Assessment," Eric Digest 320116, 1989.

McDonald, F., "The Problems of Beginning Teachers: A Crisis in Training," volume 1 in a series, *A Study of Induction Programs for Beginning Teachers* (Princeton, NJ: Educational Testing Service, 1980).

McGlynn, Angela, "Hispanic Women, Academia and Retention," *Hispanic Outlook* (February 13, 1998): 12.

McKenna, Eileen, "Gender Differences in Reading Attitudes" (master's thesis, Kean College of New Jersey: May 1997).

McLaughlin, Milbrey W. and Lorrie A. Shepard, *Improving Education Through Standards-Based Reform* (Washington, DC: National Academy of Education Panel on Standards-Based Education Reform, 1995).

Mellander, Gustavo A., "College-Bound Hispanics: Marking the Path," *Hispanic Outlook in Higher Education* 8, no. 12 (February 13, 1998): 4.

Menopause 3, no. 3 (1996): 172–180, quoted in *Women's Sports Facts* (East Meadow, NY: Women's Sports Foundation, 1997).

Middleton, John A., et al., "Building Systemic Change in Schooling Though Parent, Community and Staff Collaboration," *Journal of Staff Development* 14, no. 4 (1993): 14–18.

Milgram, Donna and Kristin Watkins, *Ensuring Quality School-to-Work Opportunities for Young Women* (Washington, DC: Wider Opportunities for Women, 1994).

———. "Wider Opportunities for Women: Ensuring Quality School-To-Work Opportunities For Young Women" (a working paper released in cooperation with the American Youth Policy Forum, March 1994).

Millard, Elaine, "Differently Literate: Gender Identity and the Construction of the Developing Reader," *Gender and Education* 9, no. 1 (March 1997): 31–48.

Montgomery County, MD, Department of Educational Accountability in a fax to American Institutes of Research, 1998, Montgomery County, MD Public Schools.

Moskowitz, Jay, et al., *Meeting the Challenges of a Teachers First Year: Lessons from around the Pacific Rim* (Washington, DC: Pelavin Research Institute, 1997).

Napper-Owen, Gloria E., "And Justice for All: Equity in the Elementary Classroom," in *Strategies* 8, no. 3 (1994): 23–26.

National Center for Health Statistics, in *Facts At A Glance* (Washington, DC: Child Trends, Inc., 1997).

National Mental Health Organization, *Children's and Adolescents Mental Health* (factsheet) (Washington, DC, 1997).

National Research Council, *National Science Education Standards* (Washington, DC: National Academy Press, 1996).

Nelson, Carole S. and J. Allen Watson, "The Computer Gender Gap: Children's Attitudes, Performance and Socialization. Spotlight: Gender Differences," *Montessori Life* 7 (Fall 1995): 33–35.

Nelson-Barber, Sharon and Elise Trumbull Estrin, "Bringing Native American Perspectives to Mathematics and Science Teaching," *Theory into Practice* 34, no. 3 (Summer 1995): 174–185.

Nevo, Ofra, "Career Counseling from the Counselee Perspective: Analysis of Feedback Questionnaires," *The Career Development Quarterly* 38, no. 4 (June 1990): 314–324.

Newman, Katherine S., "Working Poor: Low-Wage Employment in the Lives of Harlem Youth," in *Transitions Through Asolescence: Interpersonal Domains and Contexts*, ed. By Julie Graber et al. (Mahwah, NJ: Lawrence Erlbaum Associates, 1996): 323, 345.

Newmann, Fred M., et al., "Student Engagement and Achievement in American Secondary Schools," in chapter 1, *The Significance and Sources of Student Engagement*, ed. Fred M. Newmann (New York: Teachers College Press, 1992): 23.

Oakes, Jeannie, "Can Tracking Inform Practice? Technical, Normative, and Political Considerations," *Educational Researcher* 21, no. 4 (1992a): 12–21.

———. "Detracking Schools: Early Lessons from the Field," *Phi Delta Kappan* 73, no. 4 (1992b): 448–54.

Ocif, Jennifer and Beverly Marshall-Goodell, "Combining Mentoring and Service Learning" (paper presented at the National Conference of the Women in Engineering Program Advocates Network, June 1996).

O'Connor, Carla, review of *Between Voice and Silence: Women and Girls, Race and Relationship*, by Jill McLean Taylor et al., *Contemporary Sociology: A Journal of Reviews* 26, no. 4 (1997): 507–508.

Olson, Lynn, *The School to Work Revolution: How Employers and Educators are Joining Forces to Prepare Tomorrow's Skilled Workforce* (Boston: Addison-Wesley, 1997).

Orenstein, Peggy, in association with American Association for University Women, *School Girls: Young Women, Self-Esteem and the Confidence Gap* (New York: Doubleday, 1994).

Page, Relsa N., *Lower Track Class-Rooms: A Curricular Perspective* (New York: Teachers College Press, 1991).

Park, Clara C., "Learning Style Preferences of Asian American (Chinese, Filipino, Korean, and Vietnamese) Students in Secondary Schools," *Equity & Excellence in Education* 30, no. 2 (1997): 68–77 .

Parker, Lesley H., et al., *Gender, Science, and Mathematics Shortening the Shadow* (Science and Technology Education Library, Boston: Klower Academic Publishers, 1996).

Partee, Glenda, *Ensuring All Students Access to School-to-Work Opportunity Systems in the States* (Washington, DC: Council of Chief State School Officers, 1995).

Pedraza, Rachel, et al., *Home Grown Progress: The Evolution of Innovative School-to-Work Programs* (New York: Manpower Demonstration Research Corporation, 1997).

Phillips, Lynn, *The Girls Report: What We Need to Know About Growing Up Female* (New York: The National Council for Research on Women, 1998): 49.

Portner, Jessica, "Hispanic Teenagers Top Black, White Birthrate,"*Education Week* 17, no. 24 (February 25, 1998): 5.

Programmed Neglect: Not Seen, Not Heard, (New York: Ms. Foundation for Women, National Girls Initiative, October 1993).

Pryor, Sherrill Evenson, "Preservice Teacher Attitudes and Knowledge of Gender-Equitable Teaching Methods," in *Gender and Race on the Campus and in the School: Beyond Affirmative Action,* (Washington, DC: American Association of University Women, 1997).

Public Law 103–239, *School to Work Opportunities Act of 1994,* 4 May 1994.

Read, Carolyn Reeves, "Achievement and Career Choices: Comparisons of Males and Females, Gender Distribution in Programs for the Gifted," *Roeper Review* 13, no. 4 (1991).

Reese, Lyn, "Gender Equity and Texts," *Social Studies Review* 33 (Winter 1994): 12–15

Reis, Sally M. and Carolyn M. Callahan, "My Boyfriend, My Girlfriend, or Me: The Dilemma of Talented Teenaged Girls," *The Journal of Secondary Gifted Education* 7, no. 4 (1996): 434–446.

Reis, Sally M. and M. Katherine Gavin, *Why Jane Doesn't Think She Can Do Math: How Teachers Can Encourage Talented Girls in Mathematics* (Reston, VA: National Council of Teachers of Mathematics, in press).

Reis, Sally M., and Eva Diaz, "Economically Disadvantaged Urban Female Students Who Achieve in Schools," *Urban Education* (in press).

Research for Action, Inc., Jody Cohen and Sukey Blanc et al., *Girls in the Middle: Working to Succeed in School* (Washington, DC: American Association of University Women Educational Foundation, 1996).

Ross, Pat O'Connell, *National Excellence: A Case for Developing America's Talent* (Washington, DC: U.S. Department of Education, Office of

Educational Research and Improvement, Natioanl Center for Educational Statistics, October 1993).

Rosser, Sue V. and Charlotte Hogsett, "Gender Equity in the School-to-Work Movement," in *Re-Engineering Female Friendly Science* (New York: Teachers College Press, 1997): 75.

Rosser, Sue V., "Female Friendly Science: Including Women in Curricular Content and Pedagogy in Science," *The Journal of General Education* 42, no. 3 (1993): 191–220.

———. *Female-Friendly Science* (Elmsford, NY: Pergamon Press, 1990).

———. *Teaching the Majority: Breaking the Gender Barrier in Science, Mathematics, and Engineering* (New York: Teachers College Press, 1995).

———. *Re-Engineering Female Friendly Science* (New York: Teachers College Press, 1997).

Rossi, Robert and Samuel C. Stringfield, *Education Reform and Students At Risk* (Washington, DC: U.S. Department of Education, Office of Educational Research and Improvement, National Center for Educational Statistics, 1997).

Rowe, Elizabeth and John Eckenrode, "The Timing of Academic Difficulties Among Maltreated and Normal Treated Children" (paper presented at the biennial meeting of the Society for Research in Child Development, Indianapolis, IN, 1995).

Rutter, Michael, "Stress, Coping, and Development: Some Issues and Some Questions," *Journal of Child Psychology and Psychiatry and Allied Disciplines* 24, no. 4 (1981): 323–356.

Sabo, Don, *Gender Equity Report* (East Meadow, NY: Women's Sports Foundation, 1997).

Sadker, Myra and David Sadker, *Failing at Fairness: How our Schools Cheat Girls* (New York: A Touchstone Book, 1995).

Sanders, Jo, "How Do We Get Educators to Teach Gender Equity?" in *Equity in the Classroom: Towards Effective Pedagogy for Girls and Boys*, eds. Patricia F. Murphy and Caroline V. Gipps (London: The Falmer Press, 1995): 214–227.

———. "Teacher Education and Gender Equity," *Eric Digest, ED408277* (Washington, DC: Eric Clearinghouse on Teaching and Teacher Education May, 1997).

———. "Women in Technology: Attribution, Learned Helplessness, Self-Esteem, and Achievement (presented at the Conference on Women, Girls, and Technology, Tarrytown, NY, Marymount Institute for the Education of Women and Girls, November, 1997).

———. *Lifting the Barriers: 600 Strategies that Really Work to Increase Girls*

Participation in Science, Mathematics, and Computers (New York: Jo Sanders Publications, 1994).

Sanders, Jo, Patricia Campbell, and Karin Steinbrueck, "One Project, Many Strategies: Making Preservice Teacher Education More Equitable," *Journal of Women and Minorities in Science and Engineering*, vol. 3 (1997): 225–243.

Sandler, Bernice Resnick, et al., *The Chilly Classroom Climate: A Guide to Improve the Education of Women* (Washington, DC: National Association for Women in Education, 1996).

Schmurak, Carole B. and Thomas M. Ratliff, "Gender Equity and Gender Bias in the Classroom," *Research in Middle Level Education* 17, no. 2: 47

———. "Gender Equity and Gender Bias: Issues for the Middle School Teacher," *Middle School Journal* 25, no. 5 (1994): 63–66.

Schnaiberg, Lynn, "U.S. Report Tracks High Dropout Rate Among Hispanics," *Education Week* 17, no. 22 (February 11, 1998): 7.

Schultz, Debra, *Risk, Resililiency, and Resistance: Current Research on Adolescent Girls* (New York: National Council for Research on Women, 1991): 6.

Scott, Joan, "Deconstructing Equality v. Difference, or the Uses of Poststructuralist Theory for Feminism," *Feminist Studies* 14 (Spring 1988): 33–50.

Secada et al., Walter G., eds. *New Directions for Equity in Mathematics Education* (Cambridge: Harvard University Press, 1995).

Selingo, Jeffrey, "Task Force Suggests that University of California Drop SAT as Admissions Requirement," *The Chronicle of Higher Education* 3 October 1997, sec. A, p. 37.

Separated by Sex: A Critical Look at Single Sex-Education (Washington, DC: American Association of Women Educational Foundation, March 1998).

Shakeshaft, Charol, professor, Hofstra University, New York, in a personal letter to Pamela Haag, research associate, 5 February 1998, American Association of University Women Educational Foundation, Washington, DC.

———. "Reforming Science Education to Include Girls," *Theory into Practice* 34, no. 1 (1995): 74–79.

Shanker, Albert, *Making Standards Matter: A Fifty-State Progress Report on Efforts to Raise Academic Standards* (Washington, DC: American Federation of Teachers, Educational Issues Department, 1995).

Shoho, Alan R. and Irene T. Petrisky, "The Rural School Environment and

Its Effect on Adolescent Alienation" (paper presented at the annual meeting of the American Educational Research Association, New York, April 8–12, 1996).

Shortchanging Girls, Shortchanging America: A Call to Action, (Washington, DC: American Association of University Women, 1991).

Siegel, Donna and Sally M. Reis, "Gender Differences in Teacher and Student Perceptions of Student Ability and Effort," *The Journal of Secondary Gifted Education* (Winter 1994/1995): 86–92.

Silverman, Suzanne and Alice Pritchard, "Guidance, Gender Equity and Technology Education," *Eric Digests, ED362651* (Washington, DC, 1993).

Silverman, Suzanne and Alice Pritchard, *Building Their Future: Girls in Technology Education in Connecticut* (Hartford: Vocational Equity Research, Training and Evaluation Center, 1993b).

Sklover, Beverly, "Women and Sports: The 25th Anniversery of Title IX," *Outlook* 90, no. 4 (1997): 13.

Soccer Industry Council of America (1994), quoted in *Women's Sports Facts* (East Meadow, NY: Women's Sports Foundation, 1997).

Sporting Chance Program Series, (New York: Girls, Inc., 1997): 1.

Stein, Nan, "Sexual Harassment in School: The Public Performance of Gendered Violence," *Harvard Educational Review* 65, no. 2 (1995): 145–162.

Stein, Nan, Nancy Marshall, and Linda Tropp, *Secrets in Public: Sexual Harassment in Our Schools* (Washington, DC and Wellesley, Mass.: NOW Legal Defense and Education Fund and Wellesley College Center for Women, 1993).

Steinberg, L. et al., "Negative Impact of Part-Time Work on Adolescent Adjustment: Evidence From a Longitudinal Study," *Developmental Psychology* 29 (1993) 2: 171–180.

Steinberg, Laurence, *Adolescence,* 4th ed. (New York: McGraw Hill, 1996).

Stevenson, Harold, and James Stigler, *The Learning Gap* (New York: Summit Books, 1992).

Super, Donald E., "A Life-Span, Life Space Approach to Career Development," in Duane Brown, Linda Brooks, and Associates, *Career Choice and Development,* 2nd ed. (San Francisco: Jossey-Bass, 1990), 197–261.

Supovitz, Jonathan A., "From Multiple Choices to Multiple Choices, A Diverse Society Deserves a More Diverse Assessment System," *Education Week* 17 no. 10 (November 5, 1997): 34, 37.

———. "Mirror, Mirror on the Wall: Which is the Fairest Test of All? An

Examination of the Equitability of Portfolio Assessment Relative to Standardized Tests," *Harvard Educational Review* 67, no. 3 (Fall 1997).

Swanson, Janese, "A conversation with Janese Swanson," (speech at the Conference on Women, Girls, and Technology, Tarytown, NY, The Marymount Institute for the Education of Women and Girls, November 11, 1997).

"Talent Development Middle School: Essential Components," CRESPAR Newsletter, no. 1 (October 1996).

Taylor, Jill McLean, et al., *Between Voice and Silence: Women and Girls, Race and Relationship* (Cambridge: Harvard University Press, 1995).

Teegarden and Proulx et al., *Medicine and Science in Sports and Exercise*, 28 (1996): 105–113, quoted in *Women's Sports Facts* (East Meadow, NY: Women's Sports Foundation, 1997).

"Texas May Drop All Textbooks, for Laptops," *New York Times*, November 19, 1997.

The 1996 High School Athletics Participation Survey (Kansas City, MO: The National Federation of State High School Associations, 1996).

The 1997 High School Athletics Participation Survey (Kansas City, MO: The National Federation of State High School Associations, 1997).

The Commonwealth Fund Survey of the Health of Adolescent Girls, conducted by Louis Harris & Associates, ed. Cathy Schoen et al. (New York: The Commonwealth Fund, 1997).

The D.A.R.E. Program: A Review of Prevalence, User Satisfaction, and Effectiveness (Washington, DC: National Institute of Justice, 1994).

The High School Profile Report (Iowa City, IA: American College Testing Program, 1990–1997).

Theberge, Nancy, "Gender, Sport, and the Construction of Community: A Case Study From Women's Ice Hockey," *Sociology of Sport Journal* 12, no. 4 (1995): 389–402.

Thorne, Barrie, *Gender Play: Girls & Boys in School* (New Brunswick, NJ: Rutgers University Press, 1993).

TIMSS International Study Center, *Highlights of the Results from TIMSS* (Boston College, November 1996).

TIMSS International Study Center, *TIMSS Highlights from the Primary Grades* (Boston College, June 1997).

TIMSS International Study Center, *TIMSS Highlights* (Boston College, February 1998).

Title IX at 25: Report Card on Gender Equity, (Washington, DC: National Coalition for Women and Girls in Education, 1997).

Titus, Jordan J., "Gender Messages in Education Foundations Textbooks," *Journal of Teacher Education* 44, no. 1 (1993): 38–44.

——. "Voices of Resistance to Feminism: How is This Stuff Going to Make Us Better Teachers?," *Journal of Teacher Education* (July 1997).

Trotter, Andrew, "Taking Technology's Measure: Technology Counts Report," *Education Week* 17, no. 11 (November 10, 1997): 6–11.

Tyack, David, *1990: Learning Together: A History of Coeducation in American Public Schools* (New Haven: Yale University Press, 1990).

U. S. Department of Education, Office of Bilingual Education and Minority Languages Affairs, *No More Excuses: The Final Report of the Hispanic Dropout Project* (Washington, DC, February 1998).

U. S. Department of Education, Office of Educational Research and Improvement, National Center for Education Statistics, *Digest of Education Statistics 1996* (Washington, DC, 1996).

——. *Digest of Educational Statistics 1997* (Washington, DC, 1997).

——. *Dropout Rates in the United States: 1995* (Washington, DC, 1997).

——. *Extracurricular Participation and Student Engagement* (Washington, DC, 1995).

——. *NAEP 1996 Summary Data Tables* (Washington, DC, 1997).

——. *Projections of Education Statistics to 2000* (Washington, DC, 1997).

——. *Study of School-to-Work Initiatives: Studies of Education Reform* (Washington, DC, 1996).

——. *The 1994 High School Transcript Study Tabulations* (Washington, DC, 1994).

——. *The 1994 High School Transcript Study Tabulations: Comparative Data on Credits Earned and Demographics for 1994, 1990, 1987, and 1982 High School Graduates* (Washington, DC, 1997).

——. *Vocational Course Taking and Achievement: An Analysis of High School Transcripts and 1990 NAEP Assessment Scores* (Washington, DC, 1995).

——. *Youth Indicators 1996* (Washington, DC, 1996).

U.S. Department of Health and Human Services, Office of Applied Studies, Substance Abuse and Mental Health Services Administration, *Substance Use Among Women in the United States* (Washington, DC, 1997).

U.S. Department of Labor, Women's Bureau, *Labor Force Quiz* (Washington, DC, 1996).

Vail, Kathleen, "Keeping Fernando in School: In Denver, a Bold Approach is Stemming the Tide of Hispanic Dropouts," *The American School Board Journal* (February 1998): 33.

Viadero, Debra, "Immigrant Children Succeed Despite Barriers," *Education Week* 7, no. 29 (April 1, 1998): 14.

Wagner et al., "Youth with Disabilities: How Are They Doing? The First Comprehensive Report From the National Longitudinal Transition Study of Special Education Students" (prepared for the Office of Special Education Programs and the U.S. Department of Education, SRI International, 1991).

Wagner, M., "Being Female—A Secondary Disability? Gender Differences in the Transition Experiences of Young People with Disabilities" (paper delivered at the American Education Research Association annual meeting, San Francisco, 1992).

Wahl, Ellen, *The Case for Equity and Excellence in Math and Science Education* (Washington, DC: Collaboration for Equity, The American Association for the Advancement of Science, 1997).

Walsh, Mark, "Commercial Invasion of Schools Growing, Report Charges," *Education Week* 14, no. 31 (April 26, 1995): 6.

Ward, Thomas J., et al., "Examination of a New Protocol for the Identification of At-Risk Gifted Learners" (paper presented at the annual meeting of the American Educational Research Association, San Francisco, April 1992).

Ward, Janie V., "Cultivating a Morality of Care in African American Adolescents: A Cutlure Based Model of Violence Prevention, *Harvard Educational Review* 65, no. 2 (Summer 1995): 175–188.

Ward, Kelly, "Service-Learning and Student Volunteerism: Reflections on Institutional Commitment" (paper presented at the annual meeting of the American Educational Research Association, New York, 1996).

Washington, DC. The Empower Program. Empower Program Class Descriptions, *Report*, 1998.

Wee, Eric, "Turning to Teenagers for Tech Talent," *Washington Post*, 1 March 1998, sec. A, p.1.

Wehmeyer, M. L. and M. Schwartz, "Disproportionate Representation of Males in Special Education Services: Biology, Behavior or Bias" (Gender Equity in Special Education, unpublished).

What Matters Most: Teaching for America's Future (New York: National Commission on Teaching and America's Future, 1996).

Whitley Jr., Bernard E., "Gender Differences in Computer-Related Attitudes and Behavior: A Meta-Analysis," *Computers in Human Behavior* 13, no. 1 (1997): 1–2.

Whitty, Geoff, "Creating Quasi-Markets in Education," Michael Apple, ed., *Review of Research in Education*, 22 (AERA: 1997): 1–47.

Wiberg, Mary, "The School-to-Work Opportunities Act: An Opportunity to Serve All Students." *Women's Educational Equity Act Publishing Center Digest* (Newton, MA, 1995).

Wohlstetter, Priscilla, et al., "First Lessons: Charter Schools as Learning Communities," *CPRE Policy Briefs* (September, 1997): 1.

Women and Girls in Sports (Washington, DC: Feminist Majority Foundation and New Media Publishing, Inc., 1995).

Women's Sports Facts (East Meadow, NY: Women's Sports Foundation, 1997).

Women, Minorities, and Persons with Disabilities in Science and Engineering: 1996 (Washington, DC: National Science Foundation, 1996).

Woo, Elaine, "Classroom Renaissance," *LA Times*, 4 February 1997.

Woo, Elaine, "School Success of Immigrants' Children Tracked," *Los Angeles Times*, 16 June 1997, sec. A.

Woodrow, Janice E., et al., "The Impact of Technology Enhanced Science Instruction on Pedagogical Beliefs and Practices," *Journal of Science Education and Technology* 5, no. 3 (1994): 241–252.

Yates, Miranda and James Youniss, "Community Service and Political-Moral Identity in Adolescents," *Journal of Research on Adolescence* 6, no. 3 (1996): 271–84.

Yepez, Mary E., "An Observation of Gender-Specific Behavior in the ESL Classroom," *A Journal of Research* 30, no. 1–2 (1994): 121–33.

Zaher, Sandra, "Gender and Curriculum in the School Room," *Education Canada* 34, no. 1 (1996): 26–29.

Zehr, Mary Ann, "Computer Giants Look to Students: Companies Setting Up Certification Programs," *Education Week* 17, no. 31 (April 15, 1998): 1.

Zill, Nicholas, et al., "Adolescent Time Use, Risky Behavior, and Outcomes: An Analysis of National Data" (Rockville, MD: Westat, Inc., 1995).

———. "The Life Circumstances and Development of Children in Welfare Families: A Profile Based on National Survey Data" (Washington, DC: Child Trends, 1991).

baseline measures, 132
enrollment of girls, 28-32
AP tests
 baseline measures, 132
 fee subsidies, 55
 performance gender gap, 33-36, 46-47, 55
 recommendations, 55
 test-taking patterns by gender, 26-27, 33, 46-47, 124-125
Arellano, Adele, 88
Arnold, Karen, 117
Asian Americans
 AP tests, 50
 culturally specific behaviors, 62, 122
 extracurricular activities, 103
Assessment
 alternative, 54
 goals, 2
 grades, 34-35
 NAEP tests, 35, 42
 recommendations, 55
 TIMSS tests, 42
Athletics Participation Study, 98
Authentic instruction, 66

B
—

Bailey, Susan, 76
Bendixen-Noe, Mary, 62
Between Voice and Silence, 119
Beyer, Christine, 68
Biology, 15, 28, 31, 126
Biotechnology, 125-126
Braddock, Jomills, 25
Brindiz, Claire, 84
Brownlow, Sheila, 72
Brunner, Cornelia, 72
Bully-Proof curriculum, 91
Business careers, 116

C
—

Calculus, 13-15, 28
California
 immigrant population, 123
 University of California admissions proposal, 128
California Latino-Chicano High School Dropout Prevention Project, 80
Callahan, Carolyn, 25
Campbell, Patricia, 74-76, 118
Cardenas, Jose, 103
Career choice
 gender stereotypes and, 108-110
 girls' visions of, 117-118
 inequity in, 108-110
 recommendations, 120
 schools' role, 109, 119-120
 School-to-Work programs, 111-116, 118, 120
 self-selection into traditional careers, 115-116
Career counseling and preparation, 108, 110, 115-118, 124
Careers. See also Career choice
 biotechnology, 125-126
 computer science, 124-125
 environmental science and technology, 126
 job market projections, 108, 110
 math/science courses and, 124, 126
 self-selection by gender, 109
 statistics on women in nontraditional careers, 108
Channel One, 2
Chapman, Anne, 108-109
Charter schools, 1, 129
Chemistry, 15-16, 28, 126
Chepyator-Thomson, Jepkorir, 66
Child Trends, 90
Chittenden, Edward, 75

Classroom climate
  equity and standards implementation,
    58–59, 61
  inequity in, 58–59
Cleary, Theresa Anne, 46–47
Coakley, Jay, 100
Collaborative learning,   60, 65–66
College admissions and testing, 127–128.
    See also Assessment; specific tests
College and postsecondary education
  admissions practices, 127–128
  course taking and, 16–17, 26–28, 122–
    123
  gifted and honors program enrollment
    as predictor, 26–27
Colorado
  gender equity standards, 59
Commonwealth Fund, 83–84
The Commonwealth Fund Survey of the
    Health of Adolescent Girls, 84
Community service. See Service learning
Computer certification programs in
    schools, 124–125
Computer science
  AP tests, 47, 50, 54, 124–125
  certification programs in schools, 124
  course taking, 16–17, 47, 124–127
  graduation requirements, 15
  job market and, 124–125
  prerequisites for college major, 124–125
  recommendations, 31–32
Computer technology
  classroom use, 3, 68–70, 126–127
  gender bias in software, 70–73
  gender differences, 16–17, 68–70
Computer toys, 71
Consortium for Policy Research in
    Education, 129
Corporate participation, 1, 125
Council of Chief State School Officers, 13–
    14

Course taking
  AP courses, 28–32, 128
  baseline measures, 131–132
  computer science, 16–17, 124–127
  English, 17–20, 26
  fine arts, 20–21, 30
  foreign languages, 20, 30
  health and physical education, 22–23,
    95–98
  mathematics, 12–15, 25–27, 29–31,
    125–128
  recommendations, 31–32
  remedial and special education, 24–25
  science, 15, 26, 125–128
  social sciences, 20, 30
Cultural strengths, 66–67. See also
    Race/ethnicity

D

D'Ambrosio, Melody, 62
Deficit model, 4–5
Del Portillo, Ray, 80
Delinquency, 84, 89
Demographic changes
  diversity, 1
  future issues, 123–125
  Hispanic population growth, 1, 121–122
  immigration, 122–123
  regional differences among girls, 123–
    124
  student population growth, 1
Depression
  girls' risk factor, 84–85, 90–91
  sports participation and likelihood of, 96
Dewey, John, 104
Diversity
  admissions practices and, 127–128
  individual differences, 5–7
  intra-gender differences, 5–7

NAEP scores gender gap, 35
Geology, 16
Geometry, 13-14, 29-30, 125-126
Gifted education, 26-28
Gil, Rosa Maria, 122
Gilligan, Carol, 5, 64, 119
Girls in the Middle, 99
The Girls Report, 86
Goals 2000, 2
Goss, Gail, 69
Grade retention
  baseline measures, 133
  dropping out and, 80-83
  gender differences, 80-83
  socioeconomic status and, 80-83
Grades, 33-35, 50-51
Greene, Maxine, 127

H
—

Hall, Lynne, 62
Hall, Peter, 62
Hallinan, Maureen, 25
Hammer, Patricia, 62
Hanson, Sandra, 71, 99
Haskitz, Alan, 104
Hayes, Elisabeth, 18
Health
  adolescent girls, 84, 92
  sports participation and, 24, 95-99
Health and allied services careers, 112
Health care, 84, 92
High school graduation requirements, 15
High School Transcript Study, 13
High-stakes tests. See also Standardized
    tests; specific tests
  changing admissions practices and, 127-
    130
  performance gender gap, 35, 47, 50, 54
  recommendations, 41

Hispanics
  collaborative learning and, 65
  delinquency rates, 80-81
  dropout rate, 1, 80-83, 88, 122
  gender differences in achievement scores,
    43
  population growth, 1, 121-122
  resiliency, 79-83
  teen pregnancy rates, 84, 89-90, 122
History
  gender equity standards, 47, 50, 54-55
  NAEP scores gender gap, 34-35
  women's history challenge, 69
Hmong girls, 96
Hodes, Carol, 72
Hogsett, Charlotte, 112, 118
Hollenshead, Carole, 33
Home Grown Progress: The Evolution of
    Innovative School to Work
    Programs, 112-113
Home schooling, 1, 127
Honors programs
  enrollment of girls, 28-32
  participation and mitigation of risk fac-
    tors, 88-89
Horgan, Dianne D., 64
Hostile Hallways, 84-85
How Schools Shortchange Girls, 1-3, 12,
    57, 61, 68, 81, 84, 115
Huang, Shwu-yong, 88
Hughes, Tom, 104
Hughes-McDonnell, F., 66
Humphrey, Daniel, 59
Hutchinson, Pat, 104

I
—

Identity development
  service learning and, 103-105
  sports and, 95-99

Microsoft, 125
Milgram, Donna, 112
Miller, 63
Minnesota
  girls' ice hockey, 98
Monetcel, Maria Rebledo, 1
Motivation
  resiliency factor, 88
  tracking and, 25
MTP. See Manufacturing Technology
  Partnership
Multiple-choice tests, 33, 46-47, 50, 54

N

NAEP. See National Assessment of
  Educational Progress
Napper-Owen, Gloria, 66
National Assessment of Educational
  Progress
  performance gender gap, 34-35
  race/ethnicity breakdown of scores, 36-
    41
  regional differences, 123-124
National Center for Health Statistics, 90
National Center for Immigrant Students,
  122
National Coalition for Women and Girls
  in Education, 96, 99
National Collegiate Athletic Association,
  46
National Council for Accreditation of
  Teacher Education, 75, 78
National Council for Research on Women,
  86, 100-101
National Council of Teachers of
  Mathematics, 59
National Education Association, 21
National Educational Longitudinal Study,
  81, 94

National Institute of Education
  Guidelines, 117
National Merit Scholarships, 46
National Science Foundation, 13
Native American traditions, 67
NCATE. See National Council for
  Accreditation of Teacher Education
NCTM. See National Council of Teachers
  of Mathematics
NELS. See National Educational
  Longitudinal Study
Nelson-Barber, Sharon, 67
Nevo, Ofra, 117
New Jersey
  gender equity standards, 59
Newmann, Fred, 65
No More Excuses, 122
Nontraditional careers. See also Career
  choice; Careers
  School to Work and, 111-116, 118
  statistics on women in, 108, 110
Novell, 125
NOW Legal Defense and Education Fund,
  91

O

Occupation. See Career choice; Careers
Ocif, Jennifer, 104
O'Connor, Carla, 64
Ohio
  gender equity standards, 59
Oklahoma
  School-to-Work program, 114-115
Olson, Lynn, 113
Orenstein, Peggy, 61

P

Padilla, Amado, 88

R

frequency of, 84-85

policies, 84-86, 91-92

recommendations, 93

school liability for, 85-86

Shakeshaft, Charol, 62

Shields, Patrick, 59

Shmurak, Carole, 62, 68

Shoho, Alan, 104

Slavin, Robert, 25

Social studies

course taking, 11-12, 20, 30

gender equity standards, 58-59

recommendations, 31-32

Socioeconomic status

extracurricular activity participation and, 103-104

girls' sports participation and, 106

grade retention and dropout rates and, 80-83

pregnancy and delinquency rates and, 90

remedial and special education and, 24-25

as risk factor, 83-85

student employment and, 104-105

Software, gender bias in, 68-69, 72-73

Southern Regional Education Board, 123

Special education, 24-25, 30

Sports

baseline measures, 133

effects of sports participation, 24, 95-99

female role models, 96-100

gender stereotypes, 95-96, 99-101

girls' participation rates, 96-97, 101-102

media coverage of female sports, 96

persistent barriers to girls, 95, 98, 101-102

race/ethnicity factors, 95-96

ranked by popularity, 97

socioeconomic status and access, 95-96

Title IX, 96-97, 99, 101-102

Standardized tests. See also specific tests

college admissions and, 127-130

performance gender gap, 35, 47, 50, 54

recommendations, 55-56

Standards

classroom inequities, 63-66

drawing on cultural strengths, 65-68

equity for "all students," 6-7, 63-65, 130

excellence and, 63-65

implementation, 64-66, 75-76

instructional materials, 67-70

recommendations, 78, 130

states' adoption of, 2

teacher education, 73-76

Statistics/probability, 15

Stein, Nan, 86, 91

Steinbrueck, Karen, 75, 118

Stereotypes, gender

advanced, gifted, and honors students, 26-28

career choices, 108-110, 115-118

in computer software, 68-70, 75-76

gender roles, 109

schools' role in changing, 7-8

sports and, 95-101, 104-105

Student employment, 103-104

Student population. See also Demographic changes

diversity, 1

growth of, 1

Student portfolios, 57-58

Study of School to Work Initiatives, 112-113

Substance abuse, 83-85, 91, 123

Sullivan, Amy, 64, 119

Supovitz, Jonathan, 34, 55

T

Taylor, Jill, 64, 119
Teacher Education Equity Project, 75-76, 78
Teacher training
baseline measures, 133
equity training, 2, 73-76
recommendations, 78
Teacher-student interaction
classroom climate, 61-63
implementing equity in instructional techniques, 64-66
Teaching strategies. See Instructional techniques
Technoculture, 126-127
Technology
baseline measures, 133
career choice, 108
classroom use, 2, 70-73, 125
gender differences, 70-73
tracking, 126
Teen birth rate, 89-91
Teen pregnancy
African Americans, 84, 89, 122
Hispanics, 84, 88, 90, 121-122
male responsibility, 90-91
prevention programs, 89-92
recommendations, 93
sports participation and likelihood of, 98-99
student employment and likelihood of, 103-104
whites, 84, 89, 122
TEEP. See Teacher Education Equity Project
Texas
immigrant population, 121-122
Texas Board of Education, 70
Textbooks, 68-70, 76
Third International Mathematics and Science Study, 35, 42

Thorne, Barrie, 100
TIMSS. See Third International Mathematics and Science Study
Title IX
gender bias awareness and, 106-107
reinforcement of, 106-107
sexual harassment and, 85-86
sports and, 106-107
Titus, Jordan, 74, 76
Tracking
advanced, gifted, and honors programs, 26-28
extracurricular activities, 94-95, 103-104
recommendations, 31-32
remedial and special education, 24-25, 28
students' awareness of, 25
technology and, 126-127
timing of, 25-26
vocational education, 112
Trigonometry, 13-15, 126
Tyack, David, 6

U

University of California, 128
U.S. Department of Education, 82, 94, 110, 122

V

Violence
African American youth and, 89
Empower Program, 91
recommendations, 93
in schools, 1
Visual and performing arts careers, 116
Vocational and professional clubs, 106-107

Vocational education, 2, 112
Volunteerism. See Service learning

W
—

Wahl, Ellen, 4, 57-58
Ward, Janie, 89
Washington state
  School-to-Work program, 112-113
Watkins, Kristin, 112
Waxman, Hersholt, 88
WEEA. See Women's Educational Equity
  Act
Weis, Lois, 67
Wellesley College Center for Women, 91
Whitley, Bernard, 71
Wiberg, Mary, 111
WNBA. See Women's National Basketball
  Association
Women's Educational Equity Act, 110,
  116

Women's National Basketball Association,
  101-102
Writing. See also English
  gender differences, 17-20
  NAEP scores gender gap, 34-35
  Writing section on PSAT, 46, 50, 54

Y
—

Yates, Miranda, 104
Yepez, Mary, 62
Youniss, James, 104

Z
—

Zaher, Sandra, 62

AAUW Educational Foundation Board of Directors
Maggie Ford, President
Lynne Aldrich, Development Vice President
Marion Kilson, Programs Vice President
Deborah Pavelka, Co-Finance Vice President
Wendy Shannon, Secretary
Eva Chess
Judith Horan
Gretchen Ilgenfritz
Loretta Jackson
Ruth Jurenko
Jean LaPointe
Jeanette Miller
Wendy Puriefoy
Elizabeth "Betty" Rawlins
Leila Shakkour
Florine Swanson

Sandy Bernard, AAUW President, Ex Officio
Janice Weinman, AAUW Executive Director, Ex Officio

AAUW Educational Foundation
Janice Weinman, AAUW Executive Director
Karen Sloan Lebovich, Director

Project Staff
Priscilla Little, research director
Pamela Haag, research
Judy Markoe, communications director
Susan Morse, editor
Robert Brown, Jr., production
Adam Hong, design
Gillian Ray, media relations
Lisa Cain, media relations
Kris Maccubbin, media relations
April Osajima, program and state support

The AAUW Educational Foundation provides funds to advance education, research, and self-development for women and to foster equity and positive societal change.

In principle and in practice, the AAUW Educational Foundation values and supports diversity. There shall be no barriers to full participation in this organization on the basis of gender, race, creed, age, sexual orientation, national origin, or disability.

Gender Gaps: Where Schools Still Fail Our Children

Measures schools' mixed progress toward gender equity and excellence since the 1992 publication of How Schools Shortchange Girls. Report compares student course enrollments, tests, grades, risks, and resiliency by race and class, as well as gender. It finds some gains in girls' achievement, some areas where boys—not girls—lag, and some areas, like technology, where needs have not yet been addressed.
150 pages/1998.
$12.95 members/ $13.95 nonmembers.

Gender Gaps Executive Summary

Overview of Gender Gaps report with selected findings, tables, bibliography, and recommendations for educators and policymakers.
24 pages
$6.95 members/$7.95 nonmembers.

Separated By Sex: A Critical Look at Single-Sex Education for Girls

The foremost educational scholars on single-sex education in grades K-12 compare findings on whether girls learn better apart from boys. The report, including a literature review and a summary of a forum convened by the AAUW Educational Foundation, challenges the popular idea that single-sex education is better for girls than coeducation.
99 pages/1998.
$11.95 AAUW members/
$12.95 nonmembers.

Gender and Race on the Campus and in the School: Beyond Affirmative Action Symposium Proceedings

A compilation of papers presented at AAUW's June 1997 college/university symposium in Anaheim, California. Symposium topics include: K-12 curricula and student achievement; posi-

tive gender and race awareness in elementary and secondary school; campus climate and multiculturalism; higher education student retention and success; and the nexus of race and gender in higher education curricula and classrooms.
1997.
$19.95 AAUW members/
$21.95 nonmembers.

Girls in the Middle: Working to Succeed in School

Engaging study of middle school girls and the strategies they use to meet the challenges of adolescence. Report links girls' success to school reforms like team teaching and cooperative learning, especially where these are used to address gender issues.
128 pages/1996.
$12.95 AAUW members /
$14.95 nonmembers.

Girls in the Middle: Working to Succeed in School Video

An absorbing look at girls in three middle schools and the strategies they use to meet challenges in their daily lives. Includes video guide with discussion questions, program resources, and action strategies.
VHS format/26 minutes/1996.
$19.95 AAUW members /
$24.95 nonmembers.

Growing Smart: What's Working for Girls in School Executive Summary and Action Guide

Illustrated summary of academic report identifying themes and

approaches that promote girls' achievement and healthy development. Based on review of more than 500 studies and reports. Includes action strategies; program resource list; and firsthand accounts of some program participants.
60 pages/1995.
$10.95 AAUW members/
$12.95 nonmembers.

Girls Can! Video

Complement to Shortchanging Girls, Shortchanging America. An inspirational look at programs around the country that are making a difference in fighting gender bias in schools.
VHS format/16 minutes/1995.
$19.95 AAUW members/
$24.95 nonmembers.

How Schools Shortchange Girls: The AAUW Report

Marlowe paperback edition, 1995. A startling examination of how girls are disadvantaged in America's schools, grades K–12. Includes recommendations for educators and policymakers as well as concrete strategies for change.
240 pages.
$11.95 AAUW members/
$12.95 nonmembers.

The AAUW Report Executive Summary

Overview of How Schools Shortchange Girls research, with recommendations for educators and policymakers.
8 pages/1992.
$6.95 AAUW members/
$8.95 nonmembers.

Hostile Hallways: The AAUW Survey on Sexual Harassment in America's Schools

The first national study of sexual harassment in school, based on the experiences of 1,632 students in grades 8 through 11. Gender and ethnic/racial (African American, Hispanic, and white) data breakdowns included. Commissioned by the AAUW Educational Foundation and conducted by Louis Harris and Associates.
28 pages/1993.
$8.95 AAUW members/
$11.95 nonmembers.

SchoolGirls: Young Women, Self-Esteem, and the Confidence Gap

Doubleday, 1994. Riveting book by journalist Peggy Orenstein in association with AAUW shows how girls in two racially and economically diverse California communities suffer the painful plunge in self-esteem documented in Shortchanging Girls, Shortchanging America.
384 pages.
$15.00 AAUW members/
$15.00 nonmembers.

Shortchanging Girls, Shortchanging America Executive Summary

Summary of the 1991 poll that assesses self-esteem, educational experiences, and career aspirations of girls and boys ages 9-15. Revised edition reviews poll's impact, offers action strategies, and highlights survey results with charts and graphs.
20 pages/1994.
$8.95 AAUW members/
$11.95 nonmembers.

Shortchanging Girls, Shortchanging America Video

A dramatic look at the inequities girls face in school. Features education experts and public policy leaders, AAUW poll results, and the compelling voices and faces of American girls.
VHS format/15 minutes/1991.
$19.95 AAUW members/
$24.95 nonmembers.

AAUW Issue Briefs

Set of five briefs explores gender equity issues including treatment of students, educator training, the curriculum, college admissions testing, and education and training.
1990-1995.
$7.95 AAUW members/
$9.95 nonmembers.

ORDER FORM

Name _____

Address _____

City/State/Zip _____

Daytime phone (_____)_____

AAUW membership # (if applicable) _____

Item	Circle Price Member/Nonmember	Quantity	Total
Gender Gaps: Where Schools Still Fail Our Children	$12.95/$13.95	_____	_____
Gender Gaps Executive Summary	$6.95/$8.95	_____	_____
Separated By Sex	$11.95/$12.95	_____	_____
Gender and Race on the Campus and in the School	$19.95/$21.95	_____	_____
Girls in the Middle: Working to Succeed in School	$12.95/$14.95	_____	_____
Girls in the Middle Video	$19.95/$24.95	_____	_____
Growing Smart Executive Summary and Action Guide	$10.95/$12.95	_____	_____
Girls Can! Video	$19.95/$24.95	_____	_____
How Schools Shortchange Girls	$11.95/$12.95	_____	_____
How Schools Shortchange Girls Executive Summary	$6.95/$8.95	_____	_____
Hostile Hallways	$8.95/$11.95	_____	_____
SchoolGirls	$15.00/$15.00	_____	_____
Shortchanging Girls Executive Summary	$8.95/$11.95	_____	_____
Shortchanging Girls Video	$19.95/$24.95	_____	_____
AAUW Issue Briefs 5-Pack	$7.95/$9.95	_____	_____
	Subtotal:		_____
	Sales Tax (DC, MD residents only):		_____
	International Order Surcharge (25% of subtotal above):		_____
	Shipping/Handling:		$4.00
AAUW Membership-at-Large	$35	_____	_____
	Total Order:		_____

**For bulk pricing on orders of 10 or more, call 800/225-9998 ext. 477.
Please make check or money order payable in U.S. currency to AAUW.
Do not send cash.
AAUW Federal Identification Number 53-0025390
Credit cards are accepted for orders of $10 or more.**

☐ MasterCard ☐ Visa Card #__ __ __ __ - __ __ __ __ - __ __ __ __ - __ __ __ __

Expiration _____

Name on card _____

Cardholder signature_____

SATISFACTION GUARANTEED: If you are not completely satisfied with your purchase, please return it within 90 days for exchange, credit, or refund. Videos are returnable only if defective, and for replacement only.

☐ Please send me information on joining an AAUW branch in my area (dues vary by branch).

☐ I'd like to join as a member-at-large. Enclosed is $35. (Fill in education information below.)

_____

| College/University | State/Campus | Year/Degree |

FOR MAIL ORDERS, SEND THIS FORM TO:
AAUW Sales Office
Dept. 477
P.O. Box 251
Annapolis Junction, MD 20701-0251

FOR TELEPHONE ORDERS, CALL:
800/225-9998 ext. 477

CODE: M98MFE